The Complete Beginner's
Guide to
BACKPACKING

The Complete Beginner's Guide to

BACKPACKING

RICHARD B. LYTTLE

DOUBLEDAY & COMPANY, INC., GARDEN CITY, NEW YORK

Library of Congress Cataloging in Publication Data

Lyttle, Richard B
    The complete beginner's guide to backpacking.

    Bibliography: p. 137
    SUMMARY: A guide to proper attitudes and conditioning, safety
precautions, equipment, skills, and planning for the beginning backpacker.
    1. Backpacking—Juvenile literature. [1. Backpacking. 2. Camp-
ing] I. Title.
GV199.6.L87   796.5
ISBN 0-385-06879-4 Trade
      0-385-06885-9 Prebound
Library of Congress Catalog Card Number 74–18817

For Herb and Sally Lyttle

ACKNOWLEDGMENTS

The world was younger when I began camping, and this has just led me to a sad reckoning. Too many of my early teachers, including O. E. McBride, Forest H. Cooke, Joseph A. Lowrey, Van Griggs, and William S. McCaskey, have climbed their last trail and looked at their last sunset. Too few teachers remain to take responsibility for a troublesome student who grew up with so much audacity that he has now written a book on camping. I only hope that Anson A. Thacher, Howard Bald, F. Clement Taylor, and David S. Lavender, who must carry the bulk of this responsibility, will be somewhat mollified in knowing that they have my profound gratitude. I was slow to learn, but they showed me all the right trails. What more can teachers do?

Jean Bean, Dr. and Mrs. Earl B. Fenston, Mr. and Mrs. Tony Kruse, and Dr. K. O. Haldeman gave technical assistance and research material. Edward F. Dolan, Jr., Dr. Thomas G. Aylesworth, and Barthold Fles gave the faith necessary to bring the book into being. My children, Matt and Jenny, were my best critics, and my wife, Jean, remains the best trail companion a man could desire.

To all, my sincere thanks.

CONTENTS

Chapter 1

STEPPING OUT

Is backpacking for you?

Before you answer this question, let me ask you several more. Do you like to walk? Do you enjoy hard work? Do you want to explore beyond the reach of normal vacation crowds? Does the view from a mountain pass raise your spirits? Are self-reliance and independence important to you? Do you love adventure enough to give up the comfort of a soft bed and the security of four walls and a roof?

Think about your answers carefully. You do not have to give an immediate "yes" to all these questions to become a backpacker. In fact, you may not be sure of some of your answers until after you have taken several trips. But the point is this: Backpacking is an unusual sport, involving special abilities and special attitudes. You should examine with great care your reasons for taking up such a sport.

Make no mistake, backpacking is not for everyone. Many begin simply because it seems to be the thing to do. True, it has become immensely popular. Just in the past ten years, according to the makers of camping equipment, six million Americans have become backpackers.

But the popularity of an activity is rarely a good reason for doing it. And backpacking is indeed an unusual sport. Competition has no place in it. It attracts no spectators, and while it is an individual sport, it often calls for careful cooperation and teamwork. In addition, the rewards of backpacking are so many and so varied that you may wonder if it really is a sport in the ordinary sense of the word. There are some enthusiasts who prefer to call it a philosophy or state of mind, and there are a few, I suspect, who regard it as a religion.

I could go on at length in praise of backpacking, but there are several good reasons for restraint. For one thing, there would be little room left after I finished for the practical information that you need to know. Secondly, the rewards vary with individuals so much that it would be impossible to give the whole story. And finally, the rewards will mean far more to you if you discover them for yourself.

Actually, there is one more good reason for restraint. I do not want this book to promote backpacking. If anything here should persuade you, against your better judgment, to take up backpacking, I will have done you a disservice. Your decision, as suggested by the opening questions in this chapter, must rise from self-examination. You must do this alone, without the help of your friends and without the influence of a writer's zeal.

Now, let's talk about the practical business of getting started.

FIRST STEPS

Even if you are still uncertain about backpacking as your sport, you will lose nothing by following the advice in this section. My main recommendation boils down to this—take it easy.

Far too many campers are soured on backpacking because

they begin with a trip that is much too ambitious. Unless you are in top physical shape and already have some camping experience, either from car trips or summer camp programs, you should definitely not begin with an overnight trip. You should take day trips, packing no more than your lunch and an extra garment or two in case of cold weather. Even day trips should begin modestly, particularly if you are not used to hiking and if you are not certain of your future as a backpacker.

An hour's hike is sometimes all that should be attempted on the first outing. Do not walk until you are exhausted. Remember, this is supposed to be *fun*. If a group of athletic friends leads you over fifteen miles of tough trail, it may finish you with hiking, not to mention your friends, for the rest of your life.

You can work up to those fifteen-mile trips with several short trips, each one a little longer than the one before. If possible, it is a good idea on these trips to pack more and more weight as your physical condition improves. If you have a small knapsack, you can add a camera or a full canteen to increase the load. Actually, you will need the canteen for your longer trips. I have known some novice hikers who have packed bricks and sandbags to get into condition, but I suggest that a pair of binoculars, a plastic bottle filled with orange juice, or one or two cans of soda pop will prove more useful than a brick.

After you have proven to yourself that you are able to walk ten to fifteen miles without fatigue, it is time to consider your first overnight trip. We will be talking about what you need and how to plan overnight trips during the course of this book, but your first trips should, if at all possible, be made in good weather, preferably warm weather. Snow camping takes special skills. I certainly do not recommend it for beginners. Even camping in the rain requires special skills and equipment. If you continue camping, you must learn to put up with rain, but a wet trip is a very poor introduction to camping. Do your best to avoid it.

Many beginning campers run backyard tests, particularly with cooking gear and bedrolls, before they take their first overnight trip. This is an excellent way to build confidence and ability. Even veteran campers "camp" in their backyards after buying new sleeping bags or other vital equipment. If you camp with a tent, you should definitely practice setting it up at home before you go into the mountains. Tents are often tricky. Pitching techniques vary from one tent model to the next, and even with a new tent, you may find that some vital part is missing.

Now I'm sure there are some, blessed with good health and strong bodies, who are tempted to scoff at all this talk of a slow start. True, you might well be able to hike twenty miles with a loaded pack in one day without any difficulty, particularly if you are active in athletics, but there are several other good reasons, besides physical conditioning, for a slow start.

As already mentioned, you should test equipment and in the case of boots, a slow start is vital. We will later go into detail on the purchase, care, and breaking-in of boots as well as care and conditioning of your feet. For now, let me warn you that new boots, even those that fit perfectly, are rarely kind to feet, and if you wear brand-new boots for the first time on a long camping trip, you are almost certain to have grief. The short day trip provides the vital opportunity for boot break-in.

The slow start also makes good sense economically. You can take short, overnight trips without purchasing a great deal of equipment, and these trips will help you decide what you do need to improve your kit. You can set a priority of purchases which will ease the strain on a tight budget. By watching the weather and going out for just one night at a time, you might be able to put off purchase of rain gear and a shelter for a whole season. If nights are warm, you can be comfortable in a blanket bedroll. You do not have to buy a sixty-dollar down sleeping bag to start backpacking. Usually, with careful planning, you can pack all you need for an overnight trip in a knapsack. You can put off the purchase of a forty- to fifty-dollar pack until you are ready for longer trips.

Even the he-man hiker, whether he admits it or not, can thus benefit from a slow start, and I suspect that most of the he-men, after careful thought, will admit that there is more

The right gear, a perfect day, and room to roam—what more can a backpacker ask? This pack, made by Trailwise, has slide-buckle adjustments on the shoulder straps and a padded waist belt. The waist belt, cinched tightly, puts more of the load on the hips and legs. Author's photo.

to the physical side of backpacking than simple conditioning. The beginning backpacker has a great deal to learn about his body.

YOUR LIMITS

How much can I carry?

Among beginners, this is by far the most persistent question. It is one only you can answer accurately. But there are some guidelines which might be helpful.

Growing campers are particularly concerned about carrying capacity, and they often wonder how old they must be to start backpacking. I have seen six-year-olds in family groups carrying their sleeping bags and all their spare clothes. Many nine-year-olds are strong enough to carry enough for an overnight trip. From age eleven on, two-, three-, and four-night trips are often possible.

Girls mature faster than boys, and one rule you often hear is that a thirteen-year-old girl can carry as much as a grown woman and that a fifteen-year-old boy can carry as much as a grown man. I think this is misleading. Growth rates vary so much between individuals that it is impractical to fix things to age. The weight rule is a far better guide.

This states that your pack should not weigh more than one fourth of your body weight. In other words, if you weigh 120 pounds, your pack should not weigh more than 30 pounds. If you weigh 100 pounds, the maximum pack weight is 25 pounds.

As you might suspect, not all experts agree with this rule. In fact, many say that you should be able to carry a third of your body weight. And, on top of this, there are the super packers who break all the rules. You will read or hear about campers who carry packs of half their body weight and more. Further, there is the plain fact that the type of pack you use has no small influence on the amount you can carry.

Just how do you learn your limits?

Once again, we go back to the slow start—the short hikes.

An hour's walk with a thirty-pound pack will tell you in very practical terms whether it is too heavy for you.

I firmly believe that each hiker, no matter what his age, weight, or stature, has a personal pack-weight threshold. Weights above this threshold turn backpacking into grueling labor. Weights at or under the threshold allow hiking in reasonable comfort. You can discover your threshold only through trial and error on short hikes.

Of course, there is more than pack weight involved in physical limitations. Distance, terrain, very hot or very cold weather, all make demands on your body's energy and stamina. Finding your own walking pace is very important. I devote a chapter to the subject, but again, there are no fixed rules. Pace is an individual thing which you must discover for yourself. Short hikes, day trips, and easy overnight ventures offer the best opportunity for discovery.

YOUR NEEDS

You must be in good health to go backpacking. This is obvious but it has to be said. Campers will start a trip with a toothache or a head cold. We once had to turn back on the first day of a trip when a young camper in our party complained of a long-neglected ingrown toenail. It was difficult to be sympathetic.

Thus good health is the body's first need. This means knowing how to keep your health. If you are allergic to a certain food, do not break the rules and eat that food on a camping trip. In fact, you should let others in your party know of this or any other special health problems early in the trip-planning stage. If you need special medication, bring it with you on your trip. Some people who are allergic to bee stings or react to poison ivy or poison oak take special shots in preparation for a trip.

You will carry a first aid kit, but it will do you little good unless you know how to use it. You must at least know your first aid manual thoroughly before you go camping. Better yet, you can take the Red Cross first aid course. Someday your knowledge may save a life.

If you sunburn easily, carry a good lotion and avoid shorts and sleeveless shirts. If bright sun gives you headaches, use dark glasses. Dark glasses, incidentally, are vital for snow country and for hikes along the seashore or large bodies of water, where the reflected glare can become blinding.

If you suffer headaches from other causes or have difficulty sleeping, include aspirin in your first aid kit. Aspirin also helps with cramps or aching muscles. If you are easily constipated, the situation will likely worsen on a camping trip. Include a laxative in the kit.

You must know your body's special needs. In addition, you must be prepared for unusual needs that arise on a backpacking trip. For instance, there is salt. Even in mild weather you are going to sweat on the trail. Sweating takes both water and salt from the body. Thirst will warn you when body-water levels drop, but you will not be aware of salt loss until a general weakness, and sometimes dizziness and muscle cramps, set in. You must have salt tablets. Some campers take as many as one tablet every hour when hiking in hot weather. I think this is about the maximum. Normally, you should not need more than four a day. You can buy salt tablets at any drug store.

The chapter on health and safety deals in more detail with your body's limits and needs. However, it does not cover the troublesome problem of mental health. You, of course, are sane, but at the end of a tiring hike you may find that some of your friends become cranky, even unreasonable. This is particularly true on the first day. Be sure that you keep an even temper. Your friends will usually return to normal after a brief rest and a cup of hot soup or tea.

CAMPING GEAR

Every backpacker develops prejudices, particularly about his equipment. For instance, I am convinced that I have the best pack on the market and that I made a very good choice when I purchased my latest sleeping bag. However, I am going to avoid recommending specific brands. Unless a person can test all available makes and models—an impossible chore—his recommendation does not mean much. When I do mention a brand name, you must regard it as a simple prejudice, not a recommendation.

I *do* recommend that you write for several catalogs offered by outdoor equipment manufacturers. These catalogs give you an excellent opportunity to compare products and prices. The appendix in the back of this book lists the major firms.

Even if you eventually buy your equipment from a retail store, the catalogs will provide a thorough education in camping gear and brand names. Incidentally, you will see many things you do not need, such as hatchets, folding saws, snow- and rock-climbing gear, and fashion-plate clothing. You will also see things which you want but can usually live without during your first trips. A small flashlight using penlight batteries, for instance, will help lighten your bag slightly, but for your first overnight trip you can use a regular flashlight that normally sits in some utility drawer at home. You can purchase the special flashlight later.

The catalogs will also show you things that you do need. You do need a compass, for instance, and you do need a waterproof container for matches. At the same time, the catalogs may suggest ways in which you can improvise or make your own gear. Heavy wire bent into the shape of a tall W works just as well as a stainless steel cooking grill and on your first trips you can cook in coffee cans just as well as you might with a fancy cooking kit of nesting aluminum pots.

Getting back to prejudices, as you read further you will meet more of mine. You will discover that I do not like tents and believe that those who think that camping and tents are synonymous are missing much of the fun. There are, of course, some regions, such as the Northwest, and some conditions, such as Arctic or alpine weather, where a tent can be vital. I have camped for thirty years, and I still have not purchased a tent.

However, I must admit that I have borrowed tents on occasion, and been glad that I did.

My prejudice against air mattresses has a firm foundation on years of bad luck.

Air mattresses do work for other campers. I have actually seen it happen. But my air mattress always develops a leak, almost always before the second night of any trip is half over. The most attractive theory I have heard about the air mattress is that you get so exhausted blowing the thing up that you can sleep through anything, even mattress failure. The theory, however, does not work in practice, at least not for me. I now use a foam pad, but you are free to try an air mattress. Who knows? You might enjoy years with nothing more than minor troubles.

So much for my petty prejudices. Let's turn now to major troubles, and the fine art of avoiding them.

Chapter 2

HEALTH AND SAFETY

FAMILIAR GROUND

Old-time outdoorsmen like to say that city streets are far more dangerous than mountain trails. The old-timers can make this sound very convincing, but it has one big fallacy: If the city street or the mountain trail is new and strange to you, it can be dangerous.

A city dweller can easily become confused and lose confidence when plopped down in the mountains, and we have all laughed at stories about western trailblazers who become hopelessly lost in a big city.

And so, you must be sensible about changing your environment. Be willing to admit your ignorance about a region, and take steps to correct your ignorance before you step out on the trail. Every outdoor region has its own special features, its own peculiarities. Study maps, read about the area, and talk to people who have firsthand knowledge of the region.

In some high areas there are trails that stay iced up until midsummer. Often there may be forested ground that is notorious because so many hikers have been lost there. Sometimes there may be streams that you should not attempt to cross until well past the rainy season. In the Southwest, flash floods in faraway hills can turn a dry creekbed into a torrent. There is no end to the detailed information about a region that you can learn in advance. Your knowledge will not only help you stay out of trouble, but it will also increase your enjoyment of the trip. There may be rare plants or flowers along the trail, an animal that is found only in that region, or a magic moment in spring when the air fills with butterflies. If you know about such things in advance, you can often find them.

Advance study of a region is also the best way possible to avoid getting lost.

FINDING YOUR WAY

There is nothing mysterious about a sense of direction. It is not a sixth sense, not something you inherit from a great-grandfather who panned gold in Alaska, and definitely not something that will help those who "have it" out of every possible jam. No; a sense of direction is nothing more than a collection of good habits. Like all habits, once you acquire them, you practice them without much conscious effort.

If you are keenly interested in the country the trail reveals to you, if you are curious about your surroundings, you will have little trouble developing these habits.

As a beginner, you will carry a map. You leave the map at home only after you have made several trips to a region and know it like your backyard. Contrary to the common notion, you do not carry a map for use only in case you get lost. The map helps you satisfy your curiosity. If you use it in this way, it is very unlikely that you will become lost.

For example, suppose a high peak juts above the ridges to your right as you climb the trail. The map will not only help you identify the peak, but it will also tell you how high it is, how far it is from you, and give you a bearing for telling direction. When you cross a creek, the map will tell you its name and show what course the creek follows, whether and where it forks above you, and where it flows into a lake or joins another creek below.

Maps, in other words, tell where you are in relation to your surroundings. On your first trips you will probably have to work at this idea of knowing where you are. During each rest stop on the trail, bring out the map, identify landmarks, and learn to judge distances by looking both at the map and the view before you. This will soon become a habit. In fact, before long you will feel uneasy if you cannot be precise about your position on the trail. This can be frustrating, particularly when you see a distant peak that is off your map or when you have a map that does not show enough detail. We will talk about map quality later in the book. For now it is sufficient to say that the better your map, the better your trip. You want all the detail a map can show.

Many trails have signs, giving both direction and distances, but you cannot count on signs. Thoughtless marksmen shoot holes in them and vandals tear them down. Wilderness areas, where man-made improvements are banned, will have no trail signs.

Signed or not, however, the trail is a landmark. As long as you are on a trail, you can usually place yourself on the maps. In the mountains, it is a fairly safe rule that following a trail or a stream downhill will eventually lead to civilization. Of course, on a well-traveled trail you will meet other hikers who can help you to find your bearings if you become confused.

Off the trail you can run into problems, particularly in regions such as swamps, forests, barren ground—any place where there are no clear landmarks or several landmarks that look alike. I have become badly confused in boulder-strewn lava beds where each rock looked just like its neighbor. Forests, particularly on level ground, are probably the greatest threat to novice hikers. Be cautious about entering such regions. You can mark your trail by skuffing up pine needles every thirty

This army-type compass is one of the best available for backpackers. Frequent reference to your compass and your map during the day's hike will help you identify landmarks and remain oriented. This is a small portion of a fifteen-minute contour map of the Point Reyes National Seashore, published by the U. S. Geological Survey. Author's photo.

feet or so, or leaving bent twigs or stacked rocks in order to find your way out, but normally your plans will not call for backtracking. It is best to know how to use your compass before you find yourself in the middle of a forest.

The compass needle points to the north magnetic pole. That sounds simple, doesn't it, but remember, there are two ends to a needle. Make sure the needle in your compass is marked so that you can tell which is the north end. Usually one end is silver and the other end gray. If there is any chance that you will forget which is the north end, scratch or write on a piece of tape fixed to the back of the compass "north gray" or "north silver," or whatever applies to your particular instrument.

Your compass is best used in combination with your map. The map will show you which direction to take to walk out of your difficulty. The compass will keep you walking in the right direction.

Suppose the worst happens and you find yourself lost without your compass. You left it in your pack and your pack is back in camp. The sun, if you know the approximate time of day, can give you a bearing. It rises in the east and sets in the west. Thus, the sun is particularly helpful in early morning and late afternoon. At midday, when it is at its zenith, the sun is not so helpful. If you have a watch, however, the sun can give you a fairly accurate bearing any time of day.

Point the hour hand directly at the sun. You can check this by using a twig to cast a shadow on the face of the watch. Now, a line bisecting the arch between the hour hand and twelve o'clock will point south.

If your watch is set for daylight saving time, move the watch so that the shadow falls one hour behind the point indicated by the hour hand.

Suppose there is no sun. Either the sky is overcast or you are caught out at night. The first rule is to stop walking. Purposeless or compulsive walking when you are lost only serves to tire you, and walking at night, particularly in un-

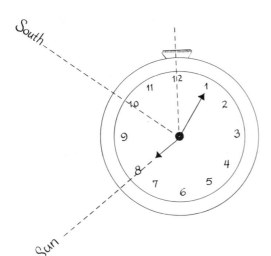

A watch can make a fairly accurate compass. Point the hour hand toward the sun. A line bisecting the arch between the hour hand and the twelve-o'clock line will point south.

familiar country, can be extremely dangerous. You can cut your-self on sharp branches or tumble to your death off a cliff. Make yourself as comfortable as possible and then take stock of your situation.

What was the last landmark you remember? How long have you been disoriented? How far have you wandered? You might be sitting within a few hundred feet of a well-traveled trail. A loud shout might be answered.

What about your friends? Are they back in camp or on the trail? When will they miss you and start looking for you? How can you help them find you? A smoky fire has brought rescue to many a lost camper. If you anticipate an air search, you should find a clearing and prepare a signal. The number three figures in nearly all calls for help. In Morse code, SOS is three dots, three dashes, and three dots. A gun fired three times, three blasts on a whistle, or three shouts will be recognized by experienced outdoorsmen as a call for help. An air searcher will be looking for three heaps of dark green brush in a light green meadow, three smoky fires, three scars of bared soil, or three flashes of light.

Rescue experts say the greatest danger to lost campers is panic. If panic sets in, you stop acting logically. So sit down, make yourself as comfortable as possible, and try to clear your mind of fears. Perhaps, when you begin thinking clearly, you will notice a slight slope to the ground that you did not see before. Hiking up the slope might lead to high ground where you can rediscover landmarks. Hiking down the slope will eventually lead to a watercourse, and it will eventually lead to civilization. There are few spots in North America that are more than a two-day walk from some outpost. Remember, trails, roads, and telephone and power lines are all man-made. They lead to civilization.

Finally, if you should rescue yourself, and your friends are still looking for you, for goodness sake, get word to a ranger or some other responsible person who can stop the search. Sitting someplace in warmth and comfort while others are scrambling over the mountains looking for you is not a good way to win popularity. This has happened. A rescue operation, re-member, is expensive. It can be dangerous.

AVOIDING DANGER

Falls are the most common cause of injury to backpackers. With a pack on your back, your body is top-heavy. Don't try to be an acrobat. Even on level ground you can stumble and suffer serious injury. Hiking too close to your companions can also lead to trouble. If one hiker stops suddenly, there may be a collision. Keep a minimum of twenty feet between hikers, and on steep grades, increase the distance. Generally, hiking down is riskier than hiking up. On a downgrade, a slip can easily turn into a long fall. Thus you should take short descending steps and be sure of your footing each time. Downhill walking is tough on leg joints. It is just as important to rest going down as it is going up.

Trails, however, are almost all constructed with reasonably safe grades. Backpackers suffer the most serious falls when they leave the trail.

You are not a rock climber. Maybe you will take up this specialized sport later on, but you must have training and special equipment to climb rocks safely. And you should not take up rock climbing until after you have built confidence and ability as a backpacker. Make sure you have a good reason to leave the trail.

A shortcut is not a good reason. Nearly always, what looks like a shortcut really isn't. You may find yourself knee deep in a swamp or faced with a hidden gully which you must detour. At best, you will probably end up on terrain too steep for safe backpacking. Trails are laid out as the shortest, safe route. Stick with them. Short-cutting a switchback trail, de-signed to ease the grade, not only puts you on steep ground, but also your track and the tracks of other impatient hikers who follow you will cut a scar that will cause erosion. Cutting switchbacks is thoughtless, the sign of a novice hiker. If you have to leave the trail to take a photograph, examine a wild-flower, or track an elusive wren—all good reasons, by the way —drop that top-heavy pack first. Of course, you must guard against getting lost, but there are other special hazards. A slope of loose rocks is the most deceptive. The slope may look stable, but your weight may be enough to start rocks tumbling. You can become part of an avalanche, and that is an experience few can survive. Snow and ice present a more obvious danger, particularly on sloping ground. It does not take much of a slope, incidentally, for ice to bring about your downfall. You should have snowshoes to walk any distance through snow, and you should have an ice ax and special spikes that buckle to the boots (called *crampons*) for ice travel. Unless you carry this gear and know how to use it, stay clear of ice and snow. If a mountain pass is blocked by snow, do what experienced campers do— turn back.

After falls, the next biggest threat to your safety is unexpected change in the weather. Actually, in high altitudes, quick changes are common. You should expect them. Of course, some regions of the country have more stable weather patterns than others. You can usually, but not always, be guided by the local "experts." I once followed poor advice and was caught in a snowstorm with summer gear and clothing. You can be sure that that will not happen to me again.

Cold can kill you, and if there is a wind blowing, this does not have to be sub-zero cold. The wind robs your body heat and brings on chill far quicker than still air. Once your body is chilled—that is, once it cannot manufacture heat fast enough to replace what is being lost—you are in serious trouble. When you are hiking along the trail, burning up energy and losing heat, this trouble can come upon you with little warning. In fact, backpackers have popularized the medical term— "hypothermia," the slow but dangerous loss of body heat. The first symptom usually comes after you stop hiking. You begin to shiver uncontrollably. You can drink hot drinks, crawl in your sleeping bag with all your clothes on, and still shiver. Campers have died of this condition. Others have shivered for hours before the body-heat balance returned to normal.

In severe cases, shock poses an additional threat. Obviously, you want to prevent even a mild case of hypothermia.

In cold temperatures, particularly if there is a cutting wind, use all your spare clothing, if necessary, to keep warm. If your clothing is not adequate, stop and seek shelter. Do not be trapped by the notion that you can hike to keep warm—the consequences of that can be dire.

A sudden rainstorm is usually more inconvenient than dangerous. If you have proper rain gear, and if your pack is waterproof, you can continue hiking in rain. Just be extra careful of your footing. If there is the possibility of wet gear, however, stop and make shelter. In the mountains, summer storms are usually brief. You can continue in a few hours, and the stopover will save you the grief of a wet sleeping bag. A down bag is slow to dry, and the wet down has little or no insulating ability.

Lightning is a spectacular thing to watch, but avoid becoming part of the show. Do not stand on an exposed ridge during a lightning storm. Avoid large, isolated trees, pinnacles, or other prominent points that attract lightning bolts. Standing beneath an overhanging cliff or in the mouth of a cave invites disaster. The bolt can travel down the wet face of the cliff and continue through your body to the ground. The general rule during a lightning storm is to keep a low profile by sitting or lying down, and keep clear of high, exposed places.

Two other common hazards campers must guard against are sharp instruments and fire. You carry a pocket knife or perhaps a sheath knife with you, and you also carry the ability to make fire.

One father I know, a doctor, by the way, forbids anyone in his family to whittle on a camping trip. This is a good rule. A knife can slip and gash a finger or palm all too easily. Even when used in necessary camp chores—cutting rope, shaving tinder for a fire—a knife must be treated with respect. Incidentally, a knife is certainly necessary, but you will be surprised at how seldom you use it.

Obviously, you know enough to avoid fire, but accidents will happen, particularly when pots are balanced precariously on a

The little items often have big importance in a backpacker's kit. The flashlight is just four inches long. The waterproof match container at the left is less than three inches high, and the snake bite kit is less than two and a half inches long. Each of them could save your life. The tape on the switch of the light prevents it from being nudged on in the pack. The items are pictured on a U. S. Forest Service map. Note the absence of contour lines. Author's photo.

makeshift grill or when there are too many campers trying to help the cook. If a hot pot falls from the fire and spills scalding water on your foot, it can put you out of action. Even picking up a hot pot thoughtlessly with your bare hand can rob you of pleasure for the rest of your trip.

You can damage clothing easily with a fire. A wayward spark can burn through a jacket as you wear it, but the damage occurs most commonly in drying wet clothes. If you hang anything near a fire to dry, keep your eyes on it. Burned socks are useless. A hole in a sleeping bag will not only cause discomfort through the remaining nights of your trip, but will also be costly to repair.

What about wild animals? They are just that—wild. They are afraid of you and want to avoid you. In fact, it is so unusual these days to see a wild animal in his natural habitat that if you see one, the event will certainly be a high point of your trip.

Two conditions make animals dangerous. One occurs when they become sick. The other occurs when they become semi-tame.

All warm-blooded animals can contract rabies, a disease that is almost always fatal to man. Members of the dog family and rodents are the most common carriers. If you should see a fox, coyote, or skunk, all nocturnal animals, wandering about during the daylight hours, suspect rabies. Any animal which acts strangely, appears to have lost its natural fear of man, or is unsteady on its feet might have rabies. Obviously, you must stay well clear of these animals. If you are bitten or have any contact with a sick animal, see a doctor as soon as possible.

A trapped animal can rouse both your sympathy and your anger, but no matter how you feel, do not try to free a trapped animal. A creature in fear and pain will bite. Your most effective protest against trapping is in the marketplace. Don't buy clothing with wild-animal fur.

The semitame animals of the outdoors have caused most of the unfavorable publicity for the entire animal kingdom. Bears that can count on handouts from sightseers and live by raiding camp garbage cans have little fear of man. If there is food available in camp, they will come and take it. Don't try to stop them. Better yet, make sure your camp has no food scraps around to attract bears, and that your food supply is cached overnight. Caching food is a camp skill we will discuss later.

Deer that beg for handouts, a common sight in many national parks, are deceptively dangerous. Their hooves are sharp, and if they become impatient they will lash out with a hoof, causing serious injury.

Feeding wild animals interferes with nature's balance. In areas with large camping populations, animals can develop a dependence on handouts. Too many animals can collect in one area. What happens to them when the camping season ends? Starvation and sickness are all too common.

Chipmunks and squirrels can play havoc with your food supply. They have been known to chew through tents to get into the groceries. Cute as the rascals may be, you must discourage them by caching food at night.

What about snakes? A great deal has been written about rattlesnakes. Some of it is nonsense. A rattlesnake will not attack. It bites only when surprised or cornered. A rattlesnake will not go on living until sundown, as some who have tried to kill them claim, and a rattlesnake bite, though certainly serious, is rarely fatal.

The rattlesnake is the most common, most widely dispersed poisonous snake in North America. In fact, about thirty-four hundred rattlesnake bites are reported each year—quite a large number—but only sixty (less than two percent) of the victims die, and doctors who treat cases say that most of those who die are either very young or very old, and in addition, their deaths are often the result of shock.

The rattlesnake has one very commendable feature. It rattles when alarmed. The noise is unforgettable, like the hiss of escaping steam. If you hear this noise in tall grass or in some other location where you cannot see the snake, simply stand still. Give the snake a chance to retreat.

Unfortunately, the rattlesnake likes to sleep during the day. Favorite spots are a shaded ledge, the ground beneath a log, thick brush, and tall grass. In snake country, avoid putting your feet or hands into a blind spot. When you cross a log, step first on top of the log. Don't just swing one leg over without being able to see the ground beyond. If you must walk through brush or tall grass, carry a staff and work it back and forth ahead of you. A snake warned of your approach will rattle and move away.

There are other, more dangerous snakes in North America, but they are not widely distributed. The red-, yellow-, and black-banded coral snake, for instance, lives only in desert regions of Nevada and Arizona, and the cottonmouth or water moccasin is found in swampy regions of the South—hardly the best regions to begin backpacking.

Insects generally are more of an annoyance than a danger. There are a few exceptions. If you are allergic to bee stings, you must take precautions. Some campers have a doctor give them a precautionary shot before they start a trip. Others carry medication with them. If you have or suspect an allergy, consult a doctor before you start your trip.

Scorpions can give painful stings, but there are just two varieties that are deadly, and they are limited to the Arizona desert.

In brush, ticks can be an annoyance. After walking through brush, inspect your skin and clothing and remove the pests before they have a chance to burrow into your skin. If a tick should get a grip on you, bathe him with rubbing alcohol or disinfectant. This will loosen his grip so you can pull him off without leaving his head in your skin. A tick's head can cause infection.

In chigger country, liberal applications of insect repellent around ankles, wrists, and waist will help reduce attack. Repellent, of course, also holds back mosquitoes, but where mosquito swarms are thick, you must also have gloves and face netting.

Reaction to poison oak and poison ivy varies with individuals and with the growing season. Avoid these plants as best you can. If you know you react, carry Calomine lotion or some other salve to reduce itching. If you have a serious problem, you can take inoculations to build immunity. Consult your doctor.

The final outdoor dangers to avoid are those made by man. Do not explore abandoned wells and mine shafts. Leave blasting caps alone, but if you see them, report their location to a ranger at the end of your trip. Do not touch animal traps.

A gun in the hands of an inexperienced hunter is a serious wilderness danger. An experienced hunter, by the way, is extremely safety conscious, and except for the opening days of a season, these are the hunters you usually meet. The opening brings out crowds. The very numbers create a hazard, and most of the accidents occur during the first few days of a season. I make it a point to speak to hunters whenever I meet them on the trail. Frankly, I want to make sure that they are aware of my presence and know where I am headed. It is a very sound idea to wear bright orange or red clothing if you plan to share the outdoors with hunters.

FIRST AID

Prevention is the best first aid. That is what we have been talking about in most of this chapter. If you can recognize and avoid hazards and develop a cautious attitude and safe habits, chances are you will have years of accident-free camping. But let's face it, accidents will happen, even to experienced outdoorsmen. You must be prepared to treat an injury. It may happen to you, to someone in your party, or to a stranger. You can suddenly find yourself faced with an emergency. How well you handle it depends almost entirely on how much you know about first aid.

You might have a very complete first aid kit in your pack, but if you do not have the knowledge to use it, the kit is useless. Lack of knowledge will lead you into stupid, even dangerous, actions, and if the victim you are trying to help has no confidence in you, your presence can well make matters worse.

Study a good first aid manual thoroughly before you start camping. I recommend the *American Red Cross First Aid Textbook,* published by Doubleday & Company. It covers everything from mouth-to-mouth resuscitation to removal of fishhooks. This first aid knowledge, incidentally, can serve you wherever you are.

You can save a life without any special equipment. If a person is bleeding severely, you can usually stop the flow of blood simply by pressing your palm over the wound. It is best, of course, to use a sterile compress, but in a serious case, the time lost in digging it out of your pack might be vital. An adult can bleed to death in two minutes. A child can die even sooner. You must act promptly to stop bleeding.

Knowledge and confidence are the only tools you need for mouth-to-mouth resuscitation, but again, you must act promptly. Few individuals can survive for more than six minutes without drawing breath. And after just two minutes, there is a danger of brain damage. You must start treatment as soon as you reach the victim.

Shock, also, can be treated without special medicine or equipment. You can even improvise a splint, to prevent movement of a broken bone, out of stout branches tied with torn shirts or bandanas as bandages. You will be surprised at how ingenious you can be in an emergency.

So why do you need a first aid kit? For one thing, it helps build confidence. Prepackaged kits include a small folder of brief instructions for various injuries. It serves to remind you what to do and settles you down in case you tend to get excited. And with a kit, you are prepared. This may sound silly, but my snake bite kit is a good illustration. I have carried it for years. It has a sharp blade, a vial of disinfectant, a thin string for use as a tourniquet, and a sheet of instructions all packaged within three rubber suction cups. I have never had to use it, and if I ever had to treat a snake bite, the chances are that I would make the necessary cuts with my pocket knife, suck the venom with my mouth, and, if I used a tourniquet at all, it would be my bandana. (For snake bite, the manual recommends a tourniquet with light pressure. For bleeding, however, a tight tourniquet is to be used only as a last resort.) Why do I carry my snake bite kit? It gives me confidence. That's the main reason. Of course, there is the chance that I might be

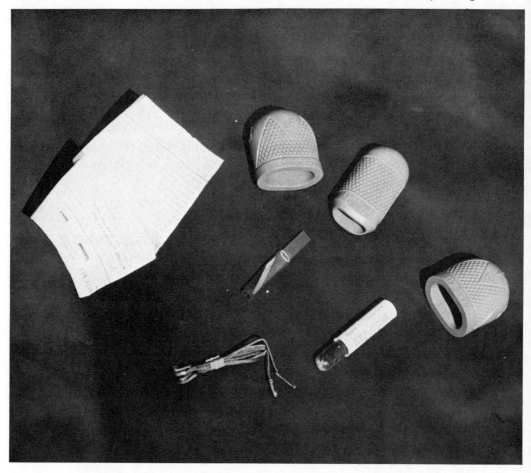

The snake bite kit, made by Cutter Laboratories, has a sharp blade, center, a string tourniquet, lower left, a vial of iodine, three suction cups, and a sheet of instructions. In snake country you should not only carry such a kit but you should also know how to use it with confidence. Author's photo.

bitten on a spot I could not reach with my mouth. Then the suction cups would be needed.

Obviously, a well-stocked first aid kit gives more than confidence. For a large cut, a sterile compress and adhesive tape make the safest, germ-free bandage. Tape also can be used to close a large cut. A roll of gauze will be needed for serious burns. An Ace bandage or adhesive tape will allow you to continue walking with a mild ankle sprain. Of course, disinfectant reduces the chance of infection of cuts and scrapes, but you must not use disinfectant on burns.

Prepackaged kits make a good beginning, but you must add to it according to individual needs. Chapstick, aspirin, a laxative, sunburn lotion, and Calomine lotion all might be needed to complete the kit for your party. Of course, some of these things can be part of your personal gear, particularly if you need them frequently.

Your personal gear should also include material for foot maintenance and repair. Many campers rely on tape or moleskin, a felt pad with adhesive on one side, both to prevent blisters on troublesome spots and to shield them if they should form. Some campers apply moleskin or tape to trouble spots before they start the day's hike, others wait until they feel a hot spot, the first warning of blister trouble.

If you get a blister, you should puncture it before applying a shield of tape or moleskin. This relieves pressure and prevents the blister from spreading. Use a needle or knife point sterilized in a match flame to make the puncture at the lower edge of the blister. Squeeze out the liquid, but do not remove the dead skin.

The two major causes of foot blisters are motion within the boot and moisture. Tightening boot laces usually reduces motion. Airing feet or changing to dry socks during rest stops will reduce moisture. Some campers carry foot powder and others carry rubbing alcohol. Both help keep feet dry, and repeated use of alcohol will harden the skin.

As with anything else, of course, the best first aid for feet is prevention, and the best possible way to prevent blisters and sore feet is to start with the right boot and a proper fit. We will deal with boots in the next chapter.

Chapter 3

WHAT TO WEAR

Boots

Feet are the backpacker's most important tools. Thus great care is vital in the selection and preservation of your boots. Purchase of good boots, in fact, is one of the three major investments you will make, the other two being the investments in your pack and your sleeping bag. Of the three, boots are far and away the most critical.

Tennis shoes, ankle-high sneakers, and light walking shoes will not give your feet the protection they must have on an extended hike. These second-rate shoes might serve on a short, overnight trip, but even then your feet are liable to protest. Light shoes give little protection against wet and cold, and remember, your feet must not only carry your body weight but also the weight of your pack. They need all the care and support you can give them.

A top-quality hiking boot such as this will cost forty to fifty dollars a pair, but the more you spend the more mileage and the more comfort you can expect for your investment. Your feet deserve the best. Courtesy of Todd's.

You want a boot at least ankle-high, with leather tops and sure-grip bottoms. Where should you buy them?

THE BOOT MARKET

The best place to buy boots, particularly for the first time, is a store that specializes in outdoor equipment. Not only will it have a wider selection than the ordinary shoestore, but more important, you can almost always count on being served by a knowledgeable salesman.

Tell the salesman where you plan to hike, what kind of weather you expect, and how much you can spend. Do not expect to spend less than eighteen dollars for a pair of new hiking boots.

Yes, good boots are expensive. Some sell for forty dollars and more, but here is another advantage in taking your business to a specialty store. Many of them take old boots in trade and thus have used boots on stock for sale or rent. If you find a pair of used boots that fit, you might have a bargain at half to two thirds of the price of new boots. Make absolutely sure, however, that the boots fit your feet as well as your budget. If your feet are still growing and you purchase boots at a specialty store, usually you can take them back next season and receive credit on the purchase of new, larger boots.

If there is no specialty store in your area, you can purchase boots by mail after sending to one of the suppliers listed in the appendix at the end of this book for a catalog. Give your shoe size with your order, but also be sure to include a tracing of both feet. Shoe sizes and boot sizes do not always coincide. The tracing is the key. Allow plenty of time for purchasing by mail. If the first boots do not fit, send them back and ask for a size smaller or a size larger as necessary.

If you do not have time to order by mail, you can seek boots in a regular shoestore. Most large stores carry a line of hiking boots, but unfortunately few of the salesmen there are specialists. You must be your own expert.

There are basically two parts to a boot, the upper and the bottom. Let's consider them separately.

THE UPPER

The upper of a hiking boot, that portion from the sole up, should be made of leather, either cowhide or horsehide. Leather molds to your foot shape with wear. It breathes—carrying off heat and letting in air, and has, at the same time, good insulating properties. No other material yet invented can match leather for hiking boots. Rubber and rubberized canvas uppers might make a fine boot for snow, mud, or trout streams, but such materials should be avoided in a hiking boot.

The top of the upper should be five to six inches high. In other words, just high enough to cover the ankle. A boot that laces higher than the ankle will restrict the action of this important joint and interfere with the flexing of the muscles in your calf. Furthermore, high-topped uppers have a way of sagging into blister-making wrinkles.

The better the boot, the fewer the seams in the upper. Most quality hiking-boot uppers are made from one piece of leather with the joining seam either at the heel or on the side of the ankle. Seams are the first places to let in water, the first places to give way to strain, and thick seams will often chafe and cause blisters.

Though design varies greatly, there are generally three types of upper construction—unlined, lined, and padded.

An unlined upper is simply one thickness of leather. This construction is common in many work boots. There are variations, however, that serve to strengthen the boot. These are reinforcing layers, a second thickness usually found at toes and heels of the boot. Layers on the outer surface are called caps. Those stitched or glued inside are called counters. Ridges, lumps, or bulky stitching that can be detected by feeling inside boots where counters or caps are joined are all signs of poor workmanship. All can cause trouble on the trail.

A lined upper is simply two thicknesses of leather, the outer shell and the inner lining. In a well-made boot, the lining will cover all stitching and seams, thus shielding your tender foot from chafing and blisters. In addition to the extra protection and support you get from two thicknesses of leather, this construction allows the use of a tough outer shell and a soft inner lining.

The padded upper is built with layers of foam rubber or similar material between the inner and outer layers. Obviously, this upper is very kind to feet, and in cold weather the layer of foam rubber provides excellent insulation. It is this insulating property of a padded upper, however, which causes criticism. On a summer hike or on a hike over desert trails, the padded upper can become intolerably hot. If you plan hot-weather hiking, avoid the padded upper.

What about leather itself? It has two sides. The outer side, once the hair is removed, is smooth. The inner side is rough and fuzzy. It has the appearance of suede. Actually, suede leather is made by splitting a hide and is thus just a half thickness, not the stuff that should be used in hiking boots.

Uppers come either with the smooth side out or the rough side out, and there is endless debate about which is best. Smooth-boot owners will claim that their uppers are easier to waterproof. Rough-boot owners say that their uppers stand up better to scuffing and general wear. Actually, it all comes down to personal taste. If you like color, the rough side of leather does show off dyes very well. Incidentally, dyes do not affect the quality of leather.

Great variation in upper design can be found at the opening—the laced gap that lets you slide your foot into the boot. The tongue lies between the gap, and its purpose is to keep out dirt and water and to shield the foot from the laces. Tongues that are connected to the main body of the upper with a loose fold of leather along each side will do a better job of keeping dirt and water out of your boot. This loose fold, however, adds weight and bulk, and boot designers offer many alternatives. There are boots with split tongues, overlapping tongues, and tongues that are attached just partway up the opening. From the variety, I suspect that the designers have not yet found the answer. You must make your selection pretty much by feel. If the boot feels right when you lace it tight, and there is an attaching fold at least halfway up the tongue, you cannot go too far wrong.

Laces are attached to the side of the opening either by eyelets, hooks, or "D" rings. The purpose of the hooks, and, I suppose, the D rings as well, is to ease lacing with cold fingers. Often a boot will have eyelets along the lower half of the opening and hooks along the upper half. Hooks will sometimes snag on brush and can be bent or broken against rocks. Do not throw your boots away because of a broken hook. It can be replaced in any good shoe shop. Incidentally, the hooks should be attached to the leather with two rivets. If possible, avoid boots with single-rivet hooks.

Unfortunately, chances are your new boots will not have adequate laces. The best by far are ⅛-inch nylon, sometimes known as ski laces. Leather thongs, once considered tops, will stretch and do not last as long as nylon. The only criticism I have heard of nylon is that it tends to slip, so the laces move off center. This can easily be fixed by centering the lace and knotting it around the bottom two eyelets. If your boots come with cotton laces, replace them at once with nylon.

THE BOTTOM

Your choice of boot bottoms is simpler. Obviously you do not want leather soles for hiking. Leather soles might serve well for dress shoes but on a rocky trail they will slip and slide like ice skates. Composition rubber and plain rubber, certainly better than leather, are not adequate for long hikes, mainly because they cannot take the beating you will give them. What you want is a bottom made of a synthetic rubber known as neoprene, which is manufactured almost exclusively under the trade name of Vibram. These should have a pattern of cleats on both the heel and the sole.

There are three grades of synthetic rubber. The poorest is taffy-colored, and it is usually identified as Roccia. It wears little better than real rubber. Next best is black, which is harder; usually it's called Montagna. It has a black label. The best and hardest is also called Montagna, but it has a yellow label inset in the instep. Soon, I understand, the manufacturers will do away with these three grades and produce only the top material. This will make your selection even easier.

If you have a pair of sturdy, comfortable boots, you can have a shoe shop give them Vibram bottoms. You are sure to be happy with the results, and so will your feet and your budget. The boots will last through long and hard usage.

There are many different cleat patterns, and it is impossible to say whether one pattern is better than another, but in all soles the cleats should be tapered. This reduces the tendency for rocks to lodge in the spaces between cleats. A small rock stuck between cleats can cause a slip.

Above the Vibram sole, hiking boots have a foundation layer of leather. Often there are two layers of leather, and some heavy-duty shoes have a reinforcing plate of metal between layers. This metal plate, perhaps necessary in special rock-climbing boots, is a liability in a hiking boot because it adds excess weight. No matter how the boot bottoms are designed, there should be about a half inch of material between your foot and the ground.

The bottoms are connected to the uppers of a hiking boot in two ways—the exposed welt and the hidden welt. The welt is nothing more than the line of stitching connecting the upper with the first foundation layer of the bottom. When the leather of the upper is turned in before stitching, the welt is hidden.

When the leather is turned out, the welt is exposed. At the moment, the hidden-welt construction seems to be the most popular in hiking boots.

WEIGHT

It is said that a pound of shoe weight is equal to five pounds of pack weight in terms of physical exertion. Thus, you want to avoid a boot that is heavier than you need. Rock climbers need heavy boots—at least five pounds a pair for an adult male climber—but you do not need such mighty armor for hiking. Your boots should weigh about three and a half to four pounds a pair, and women's and children's boots will be even lighter. At the same time, unless you have very small feet, you should be suspicious of any pair of boots weighing less than two pounds. There are many cheap imitations of hiking boots made with cleated rubber bottoms and suede uppers. They are feather light, priced around ten to twelve dollars, and look like the real thing. Avoid them.

We have gone into a great deal of technical detail about boots, but we have still to cover the most important matter of all—good fit. Before we discuss this, however, we must consider another vital subject.

STOCKINGS

The main purpose of stockings is to protect your feet, thus you want a thick stocking of wool, Orlon, or wool-Orlon combination. Cotton stockings absorb sweat and give a wet, clammy feeling at best. At worst they will induce blisters. No matter what the material, avoid a stocking with a coarse, open weave. After hiking for a few miles, such stuff will make your feet feel and look as if they have been branded by a hot screen.

Carry two pairs of socks to make sure you always have a dry pair in your pack. It is important to air out and dry socks after use. If you feel it is just as important to wash them after each use, make sure there is enough time and enough warm weather to have them dry when you need them. A dirty sock will do far less damage than a wet one.

Some backpackers wear two layers, an inner sock of fine weave and an outer one of heavier stuff. Experiment with this if you wish. It may sound fussy, but you cannot be too fussy where your feet are concerned. Besides, it does seem to work well for some hikers.

No matter what kind of sock or combination of socks you settle upon, you should have a good thick pair on your feet when you get ready to try on those all important new boots.

THE RIGHT FIT

The time you spend in searching for a boot of proper fit is probably the most important time you will spend in pursuit of this sport. Do not rush. The salesman, if he knows his business, will encourage you to be patient.

First of all, you want a boot that feels right. What feels right? That is a personal matter up to you and your foot. Often you will say, "Ah . . ." as you slip your foot into the boot. There is a certain natural comfort that makes this boot different from the others you have tried on.

Now put the boot to a test. With the laces loosened, jam your foot forward as far as it will go. You should be able to slide a finger between your heel and the heel of the boot, even two fingers if you are dealing in large boot sizes. Next, lace the boot tightly, with your heel seated back against the leather.

The main area of tightness should be under the lower portion of the laces, around the ball of the foot and perhaps the forward part of your arch. There should be ample room to wiggle your toes, all of them.

There should be no pressure points at any place in the boot. Don't buy boots with the theory that usage will cure a bad fit. They should fit well from the beginning. If you find a boot that fits well except in one spot, you can mark the spot and have the leather "punched out" at a ski-boot shop. This is a special leather-stretching process. I recommend it only as a last resort. Boots that feel comfortable but have a general looseness around the bottom can be made to fit more snugly with insoles. It is best if you do not have to use them, but sometimes insoles are the only answer.

By now it should be obvious why you should be wearing thick socks when you try on your boots. Thin, dress socks will mislead you badly. If you find yourself wearing dress socks at the shop, it would be a good time to purchase your hiking socks before you start trying on boots. Some salesmen will lend you socks for a fitting, but you should not expect this special service.

CARE AND BREAK-IN

You will want to waterproof your boots as soon as you get them home, but before you leave the store, find out what waterproofing compound is recommended. Leather is cured in two ways—by natural plant extracts or by chrome compounds. The natural process, sometimes called oil tanning or curing, produces a leather that takes an oil-base conditioner. Chrome-cured leather takes a silicone-base wax for conditioning and water-proofing. Use of silicone on naturally cured leather can damage it. Use of oils on chrome-cured leather can damage it. Use the right stuff.

After a day's hike, if your boots are wet, do not dry them out over the campfire. Heat will cook the leather, drive out the oils, and destroy the cell structure. You will end up with a pair of hard boots that will soon start to crack and fall apart. Let your boots dry inside the tent or under a tarp shelter. Dry your socks over the fire. Your boots may still be damp in the morning, but the dry socks will protect your feet, and you will be surprised at how quickly your boots dry out on the trail.

Before you put your boots away after a trip, remove caked mud and apply fresh waterproofing compound if it is needed. Store the boots in a dry place, but do not leave them near a heater or hot-air vent. If you will not be using the boots again for several weeks, stuff newspapers into them so that they keep their shape.

Brand-new boots, no matter how well they fit, will be stiff and can cause blisters and great discomfort if not broken-in. Also, your feet have to grow used to them. The break-in process, in fact, is in part a feet-toughening process.

Wear the boots on short hikes. Wear them to school or around the house. You should be able to wear them on a five- or six-mile hike without discomfort before you take them on their first backpacking trip. This is very important.

If you are rushed and do not have time for this break-in, you can try hot tap water. Fill each boot with hot tap water, and let the water stand no more than half a minute before dumping it out. Then put the wet boots on and wear them. (I have never had the nerve to try this, but I'm told it works. You should not try it unless there is no other way.)

From the Feet Up

You will want several layers of clothing for backpacking. One reason for this is that temperatures can rise or drop several degrees in just a few minutes, particularly in thin mountain air. Stepping from sunlight into shadow can bring a drop of twenty degrees or more. Another reason is that packing a load of gear is hard work. Your body will be hot as you hike, but when you stop you will cool off fast. There is a real danger of chill. Once you start shivering, it is very hard to stop. You want to prevent this before it happens by putting on a warm layer of clothes as soon as you stop hiking. Still another reason for having several different garments is that some will be needed for specialized purposes such as shedding rain or cutting wind.

Let's discuss the layers from the inside out.

UNDERWEAR

If possible, wear the kind of undergarments you wear in daily life. They are what you are accustomed to, and you do not run the risk of having something that bunches or binds. However, you should avoid flimsy stuff, and if you expect cold weather, you may want to consider long johns. Long underwear is ideal for frosty nights. Pajamas are excess baggage on a camping trip, but long johns make sense because they can do double duty either as sleepwear or daytime wear. You must be sure, though, that you have a good fit.

The conventional shoulder-strap undershirt is not as well suited for backpacking as a T-shirt. The T-shirt provides a better foundation under pack straps, and on hot days it can serve as your only top garment.

SECOND LAYER

A pair of jeans, long enough to cover your boot tops by at least two inches, makes an ideal trouser for almost all hiking conditions. On a cold hike, army-type woolen trousers or heavy whipcord may suit you better, but in the heat of the day when you're working hard under your pack this thicker material can become very uncomfortable. Jeans, with long johns in reserve for falling temperatures, make a more versatile combination.

Many hikers like to don shorts as soon as the sun comes up. Shorts can be comfortable, but be alert for sunburn, and never go backpacking with shorts alone. You will need the long trousers for cold days, for hiking through brush, and for evening wear. Mosquitoes and gnats can be murder on bare legs, and long trousers are supposed to give protection or at least peace of mind when hiking through snake country.

For a top garment, I recommend a long-sleeved shirt of heavy cotton. You may prefer short sleeves, but these lack versatility. You can always roll up a long sleeve in hot weather. The shirt should have two breast pockets. I like pockets with button-down flaps.

THIRD LAYER

You have a fairly wide choice here—a wool or Orlon sweater, a thick, woolen shirt, or maybe even a sweatshirt will serve. The main idea is to have something for extra warmth. On a cold trip a sweatshirt will not do the job, but it can be just right for summer evenings.

If you decide on a sweater, avoid a turtleneck. It may look stylish, but it does not fit in well with the layer system.

FOURTH LAYER

For the ultimate in comfort, you will want a down jacket. The jackets with hoods, drawstring waist ties, and about twenty ounces of down filling will cost sixty dollars or more. Normally you will not need this much jacket. You can get by with what the catalogs list as down undershirts or sweaters. They have knitted or elastic cuffs and no hood. They contain about six ounces of down filling, and cost from twenty-five to thirty dollars. They will do the work of two heavy sweaters, and their light weight and small volume when packed make them ideal for backpacking.

If you cannot afford this luxury at first, I suggest an extra sweater combined with a woolen shirt for the fourth layer. This will add both bulk and weight to your pack, and make you fully appreciate that down garment when you finally can afford it.

This down jacket, referred to by suppliers as a down sweater or under-shirt, makes an adequate top layer for all but extreme cold. When packed, it takes up less space than a loaf of bread. Author's photo.

A parka, with twice the amount of down stuffing contained in the sweater, will keep you warm in Alpine or Arctic weather. Unless you are cold-blooded, however, it will be more than you need for summer evenings. Notice the detachable hood. Courtesy Alpine Designs.

FIFTH LAYER

Finally, you will need a combination rain jacket-windbreaker. These are listed in most of the catalogs as "shells" because they have no lining. Most are made of lightweight, treated nylon. Yours should have a hood. I like the hoods that tuck away in a Mandarin-type collar, ready for use in rain or wind.

What about hooded ponchos as a substitute for the fifth layer? Ponchos are fine rain garments on the trail, and they can serve well as emergency shelters, but they are awkward to wear in camp, especially around a fire, and they can be frustrating in a stiff wind. Though ponchos have their virtues, do not consider one as a substitute for a hooded, waterproof windbreaker.

Hats

I once saw a backpacker in a silk top hat. It looked classy, but it was very impractical. You want head gear that will not be knocked off or nudged over your eyes by your pack, and you want something that will shade your eyes and protect your neck and ears from sunburn. A floppy felt hat that can be sat upon, stepped on, or crushed into your pack without loss of dignity will answer your needs nicely. A knitted cap, though hot on the trail, makes excellent sleepwear, particularly if your sleeping bag lacks a hood.

Other Items

Though clothing is a matter of personal taste, the things listed here illustrate the layer system. Be guided by this system when you select your clothes. The catalogs list such things

Down vests have recently gained popularity among campers because they retain body heat and at the same time allow great freedom of motion. They also fit in well with the layer system. Courtesy Alpine Designs.

as down vests, string underwear, ski skins (actually, just fancy long johns), and knickers. Make sure that these things or anything else you may be tempted to buy fit in with your layer system.

When you take up snow camping you will need gloves and perhaps gaiters and down booties, but such gear will be useless for summer camping.

This couple can hike through the rain all day with little discomfort. The two-piece parka-trouser combination is favored over the poncho by many campers, but some hikers who sweat readily claim that these outfits are too hot. Courtesy Alpine Designs.

This is more than a rain jacket. Though it is a shell, meaning it has no lining, the jacket serves as a good windbreaker and provides plenty of warmth in mild weather. The large pockets in this design are a boon. Courtesy Alpine Designs.

Last but certainly not least on the clothing list is the versatile bandana. Carry a large one. Carry two large ones. You may need them both. They serve as emergency hats, collars that shield the neck from sun or cold, hot pads for lifting pots, and bandages. They also help wipe sweat from your brow.

Chapter 4

BEDDING AND SHELTER

Conserving Heat

A sleeping bag's main function is to limit your loss of body heat while you sleep. Your body, provided that it is well fueled with food, manufactures heat constantly, but the production drops to its lowest level while you sleep. In addition, the cold ground, cold air, wind outside your bag and drafts circulating within, and moisture all work to rob your body heat. The best protection against these heat-robbing forces is a close-fitting envelope of dead air around your body.

How well this envelope functions is determined by the design and materials used in your bag.

A rectangular bag with excess space within allows heat-robbing drafts to circulate around your body. It is not nearly as efficient as a form-fitting mummy bag. The filling material used within the inside lining and outside shell of the envelope

This mummy bag, advertised for comfort down to ten degrees above zero Fahrenheit, contains two and a quarter pounds of down stuffing. Courtesy Alpine Designs.

A lighter bag with no hood is advertised for comfort down to thirty-five degrees. It contains two pounds of synthetic insulation. Courtesy Alpine Designs.

also has a great deal to do with the efficiency of your bag. Cotton filling mats under your body weight and tends to hold the moisture produced by your body. Fibers of synthetic Dacron and duck or goose down do not mat as readily and let body moisture escape without loss of insulating quality.

In addition, backpackers make a tough demand on filling material. It must be light and it must compress to small volume. Dacron and down meet this demand. Cotton fails miserably.

Between the two best insulators for sleeping bags, Dacron has the advantage of being about half the price of top-quality down. Also, it dries out more easily when your bag gets wet. Down, however, is lighter and compresses slightly better than Dacron. Thus a practical down bag for summer use might weigh 3¼ pounds, while a comparable bag with Dacron filling will weigh about 4¼ pounds. Remember, however, that Dacron is cheaper. You can pick up a mummy-type bag for summer use for twenty-five to thirty dollars. The down bag will cost fifty to sixty dollars.

YOUR BAG

It is possible to go backpacking with a bedroll made of two army blankets, one folded inside the other. Many budget-conscious campers have started with such an outfit and survived in comfort.

You can either sew together the edges of the folded blanket or simply fasten them with blanket pins. Roll up the blankets lengthwise in a vinyl sheet for rain protection and then tie the bedroll horseshoe-shape around your pack. Unless you are camping in very hot weather, you will probably wear most of your clothes to bed to assure a warm sleep when you use a bedroll.

Perhaps you already have a conventional, rectangular bag. It probably has cotton filling and weighs about six pounds. It too can be used for your beginning trips. The weight and bulk will be a handicap, but the bag will keep you warm through summer nights.

Though a bedroll or a conventional bag will serve for short trips in warm weather, you will eventually want to buy a bag designed especially for backpacking. Here are a few tips to help you in your purchase.

The shell and lining in most bags on today's market are made either of finely woven nylon or cotton. Nylon is lighter and longer lasting. Salesmen will usually refer to the lining in the best bags as "ripstop" nylon. Nylon, after use, takes on a smell that some campers find offensive. Cotton will not do this, but cotton has a bothersome way of clinging to you, particularly when you are wearing clothes. This restricts freedom of movement inside the bag.

Do not buy treated lining or shell material. You do not want a bag that is waterproof or water resistant because your body moisture must escape through the bag. If it does not, the filling material will soon become wet with condensation, and wet filling material has practically no insulating value.

Bag construction is important. I suppose there are still some bags made with simple, sewn-through quilt design. Avoid this cheap construction. To hold the filling material in place, the quilt makers have simply formed pockets by sewing the inner lining to the outer shell. Wherever there is a seam, there is, of course, no filler. Overlapping quilt construction covers the cold seams, but it also makes for a heavy bag because of the need to use an extra layer of lining material.

Most quality bags today are put together with some kind of baffle construction. Square, slant and V baffles seem to be the most popular.

If there is one major fault of modern sleeping-bag manufacture it is that too many are designed for Arctic or even sub-Arctic temperatures. You are almost certain to get something hotter than you need for summer camping. So make sure, unless you plan an Arctic or Alpine trip, that your bag has a zipper. Some bags come with a yard-long zipper and others come with a zipper that reaches to the toes.

Be leery of the fine-toothed zipper. Zippers with moderately large teeth are best, and they should have a draw tab on the inside as well as the outside of the bag. Steel zippers, incidentally, tend to stick more than plastic or aluminum zippers. A zippered opening, of course, makes it much easier to get in and out of your bag, and it gives vital ventilation on warm evenings. Later, if you wake up feeling chilly, it is simple to close the bag and tighten the drawstrings to close the hood around your head.

Many manufacturers rate their bags by temperatures, saying, for instance, that the bag is designed for zero-degree comfort or for thirty-two degrees or whatever. Don't be overly influenced by these claims. Your own metabolism and your normal diet have a great influence upon the amount of heat

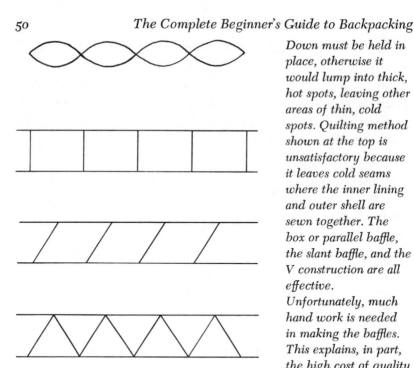

Down must be held in place, otherwise it would lump into thick, hot spots, leaving other areas of thin, cold spots. Quilting method shown at the top is unsatisfactory because it leaves cold seams where the inner lining and outer shell are sewn together. The box or parallel baffle, the slant baffle, and the V construction are all effective.

Unfortunately, much hand work is needed in making the baffles. This explains, in part, the high cost of quality sleeping bags.

your body produces. A bag that gives comfort at thirty-two degrees for one camper might be a hothouse for another.

It is a good idea to run a backyard test with a new bag. Try sleeping outside and see how you fare the night. Perhaps you will be more comfortable wearing socks and a sweater. Maybe you will find that you can sleep naked with no discomfort even on a cold night. The experience will help you in planning your trip.

SIZE

Because they are designed to be snug, fit of mummy bags is important. Growing campers, however, should buy bags that they can use for at least two or three seasons by selecting over-sized bags. It may be a little drafty the first season, but extra clothing at night and an underfold at the foot of the bag will usually remedy the draft problem. It is much easier to sleep in a bag that is too large than in one that is too small.

Most major manufacturers now make children's bags. In addition, there is the foot bag or elephant's foot. This is designed for adults who tie the bag at their waist and wear a down parka to protect the upper portion of their bodies. The foot bag works well as a child's bed, and a child can eventually grow into the parka-and-foot-bag sleeping system.

Adult sizes usually range through large, medium, and small, and there is about a five-dollar drop in price going down from one size to the next, a boon for small campers.

Both length and girth must be considered in selecting the right fit. Unfortunately, bag suppliers do not permit purchases on trial. Thus, you must make sure of your fit when you make the purchase. Many suppliers, however, do rent bags. If you are uncertain about the best size for you, rent a bag. It will cost about five dollars for a three-day trip. One night will tell you all you need to know to make the decision on size. The rental bag may be just right, or you may discover that you need a size larger or a size smaller. What you pay for the rental will be a good investment.

Don't borrow a bag from a friend. Switching bags around within a family is one thing, but sleeping bags are personal things. In addition, you cannot be sure a borrowed bag will fit properly. And there is a heavy responsibility in caring for someone else's bag. Bag care takes some special knowledge.

CARE OF YOUR BAG

One of your top concerns on a trip should be a dry sleeping bag. A waterproof stuff bag is essential if you carry your bag strapped to the outside of your pack, and many campers encase their sleeping bag in a plastic sack before putting it into the stuff bag. Bags can get wet with use, either through condensation drips or leaks from a tent or tarp or from spilled food. Spreading waterproof rain gear over your bag holds in body moisture and will turn your bag soggy during the night.

The same thing can happen if you breathe inside your bag. Keep your mouth and nose on the outside.

Trying to dry out a wet bag in overcast or rainy weather can be a very frustrating experience. Hanging a bag by a fire for a day may dry out a bag with Dacron stuffing, but it will do little good for a wet down bag, and the chance of flying sparks burning holes in the shell is a real threat. In addition, nylon will melt in high heat. If you must hang a bag by a fire, watch it constantly. The best cure for a wet bag is sunshine and dry air. You can hang a bag loosely outside your pack if the weather is right for drying. If the weather is not right, you must prepare for some uncomfortable nights until your bag dries out.

Rips or burn holes in the shell or lining should immediately be patched temporarily with adhesive tape or ripstop nylon tape. You can have nylon patches sewn on when you get home. If you notice any loose stitching during your trip, tape it and replace the stitching when you get home.

Most bags are designed with a tube of filler material behind the zipper. It blocks cold air from coming through the teeth of the zipper, but it also has a tendency to snag when you pull the zipper closed. To prevent snagging, keep one finger inside the bag between the tube and the zipper when you pull the zipper tab. A stuck zipper, particularly one that is stuck open, will cause serious discomfort. You can tape the opening shut or sew it if you carry needle and thread.

If the tab breaks off a zipper, you can repair it with a piece of bent wire wrapped with tape. A piece of string will also serve as a temporary tab.

When you return from a trip, open your bag and turn it inside out before drying it in the sun. If there is no sun, dry it indoors for at least two days before storing it. Do not store the bag in its stuff bag. Filler that is compressed for long periods loses its fluffiness and tends to retain lumps. Fold the bag loosely on a shelf or hang it over a clothes hanger.

What about cleaning? I don't worry too much about spots or stains, but if they bother you, use spot remover or simply a sponge dampened with hot water. Test any spot remover first on a small portion of the material. Lacquer thinners will dissolve nylon, but most turpentine-base cleaners are safe. Many manufacturers say that their bags can be machine washed and dried or sent to the dry cleaners. Excessive heat, however, can destroy a bag, and I do not think that the machine tumbling does a bag much good either. If you do send a bag to the dry cleaners, make sure that the establishment has experience with sleeping bags.

BENEATH YOUR BAG

A ground cover of cheap plastic—the type painters use for drop cloth is ideal—serves two purposes. It helps slow the transfer of your body heat to the cold ground and it helps keep you, your bag, your clothing, and your gear clean.

Ground covers receive a good deal of wear. Twigs and sharp pebbles poke holes in them and they gather dirt. Some campers like tough canvas for ground covers, but it is heavy and it is often hard to shake the dirt off canvas. The plastic usually lasts through a season, and it is no great financial loss when it wears out.

I like a ground cover that measures about ten by eight feet. This gives plenty of room for the gear I keep around my bag, and the extra footage is very convenient protection against brief showers that strike during the night. You simply pull the extra material over your bag until the shower passes.

Between the ground cover and your sleeping bag you will want a foam pad or mattress. This provides further insulation between you and the ground, but more important, it cushions your tender body from the hard and lumpy realities of earth. Ensolite and urethane both make good pad material and you can purchase both in thicknesses ranging from ¼ of an inch to 1½ inches. Some campers use hip-length pads, but I like the added insulation provided by a full-length pad. Also, unless you are very hardy, be cautious about pads less than ¾ of an inch thick.

As already stated, I have developed a strong prejudice

against the air mattress. Inevitably, you must huff and puff to blow these things up at the end of the day when there are not many huffs and puffs to spare. Also, inevitably, if the things develop a leak, and the best do, you do not discover it until sometime after midnight. Prudent campers who carry air mattresses also carry kits to fix them—a real bother, in my mind.

Of course, an air mattress is handy for rafting yourself across the Colorado River or simply for good sport in mild rapids of any stream, but they do not take kindly to this use. You can buy very cheap plastic mattresses which sometimes last through a night, or you can spend twenty to twenty-five dollars for the rubberized-cloth jobs, which will go through many seasons, usually collecting patches like service stripes.

Your Roof

My favorite camping roof is a star-studded sky, and I will put up with a good deal, including dew and early morning frost, to use it. Why campers squirm into the stuffy confines of a tent on a beautiful summer night is something I fail to understand, and I am convinced that tents are overrated.

So much for my views. Now let's talk about those nights when you really do need shelter.

Suppose it is raining or threatening to rain when you make camp. You want to keep yourself dry, but you also want to provide shelter for your food and clothing and your sleeping bag. I carry a ten-by-twelve-foot sheet of polyethylene called Visqueen. It is tough, .004 inches thick, and translucent. In other words, it lets enough light through to prevent claustrophobia, but will block enough sun on a hot day to throw a comfortable shade. True, this plastic tarp does not look very rustic or woodsy, but it is so versatile and reliable that you can afford to ignore its appearance.

My ten-by-twelve sheet weighs 2.3 pounds and will shelter four sleepers comfortably. Two campers can get by with a

It may not look handsome or woodsy, but a sheet of polyethylene makes perfectly adequate shelter, and it can be rigged in many different but simple ways to suit your needs. Notice how a guyline has been wrapped around a pebble that was bunched in a corner of the tarp. Author's photo.

nine-by-eight sheet, but that is about the minimum size for practical pitching.

Light nylon cord makes good guylines and you can make a "tent" peg with a ten-inch length of No. 8 wire. Bend a hook or loop in one end of the wire. I carry twenty feet of line and six wire pegs. The line gets chopped up into various lengths to suit the engineering demands of pitching the tarp in each new situation as the trip progresses.

To tie a guyline to the tarp, simply make a pocket of the material around a small pebble, wrap the line twice around this pocket, and tie it off tightly. The other end of the guyline can be tied to a rock, tree limb or tree trunk, protruding root, or, of course, to one of your pegs. I am assuming that you have a basic understanding of knots, but there is one special knot that is very handy in rigging tarps and tents. It is the guyline slip knot and it is tied like this (see page 57).

Rather than fasten your line to the tarp with a pebble, you can use a device known as a Visklamp. It consists of a small rubber ball and a piece of wire looped in the shape of a lop-

The guyline slip knot, very handy for rigging tarps and tents, is easy to tighten. Here the drawn-up slack will be taken out with a quick tug on the knot. Author's photo.

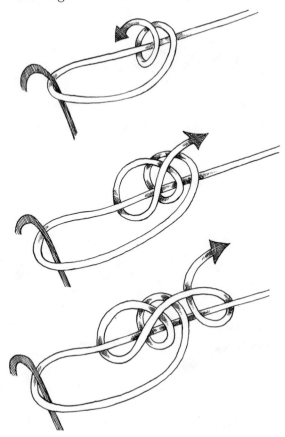

The guyline slip knot is basically nothing more than three half-hitches, two inside and one outside the tent stake loop. The knot tightens under tension on all but the slickest synthetic lines. If your knot does not hold, add another inner half-hitch.

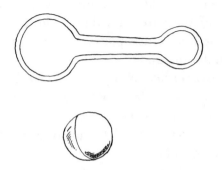

The Visklamp for fixing lines to plastic tarps is a simple device and easy to use. Bunch material around the hard rubber ball and shove the ball through the large loop of the clamp. Then slide ball and material to the small end. Tie your line to the large loop of the clamp.

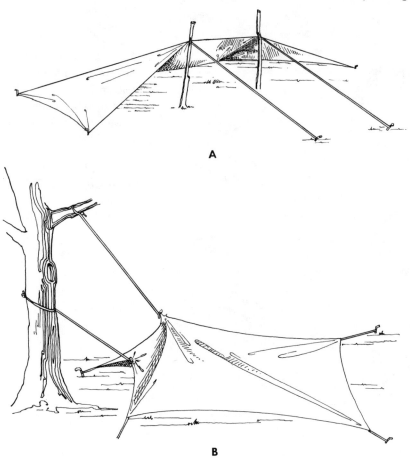

A

B

sided dumbbell. You bunch the material around the ball, slip
it through the large loop of the wire, and then slide it to the
small loop. Visklamps cost ten cents apiece. Six of them together weigh four and a half ounces.

You can rig a plastic tarp either as a wind screen, a rain
shelter, or a combination of both, depending on the circumstances. For desert camping you can rig it as a sun shade during the lunch stop. Here are just a few of the many ways they
can be rigged (see sketches A to D):

My major objection to plastic tarps is condensation. Often,
on a windy night, you must rig them with low clearance over
your sleeping area, mainly to keep out wind-driven rain, but

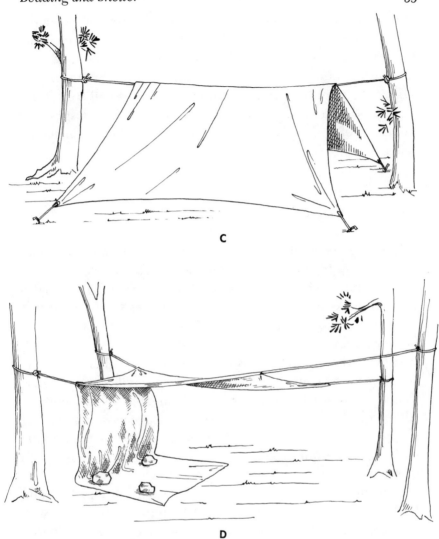

C

D

A spacious shelter (A) can be made with two branches and six tent stakes, but take care to pitch this shelter with the low side toward the prevailing wind. For driving rain, a low shelter (B) will reduce dampness around the edges of your bedroom, but you must put up with considerable condensation with this rig. A ridged shelter with the peak held up by a line between two trees (C) allows enough air circulation to hold down condensation. A combination wind screen and rain shelter (D) provides even more air. There are many other ways to pitch a tarp. Use your imagination and do not worry too much about appearances. Your goal is shelter against the elements.

also to keep a low profile so that the wind does not get under the tarp and lift it with powerful gusts. The ties will sometimes tear in a strong wind. The low rig cuts circulation and thus moisture from your body and your breath collects on the underside of the tarp. If your bag touches the tarp, it will collect this water and become soggy and uncomfortable. But despite this fault, I prefer the plastic tarp to any other shelter, including tents.

WHAT ABOUT TENTS?

The catalogs are full of tents of many designs and materials. You may be tempted to buy one, and let's face it, there are circumstances where you will want a tent. Some claim that a tent can make a difference of twenty degrees between outside and inside temperatures. I think that is a slight exaggeration, but just the same, tents offer a distinct advantage in cold-weather camping. They also provide snug shelter in strong winds. And, of course, a well-designed tent will keep you dry. Tents are also a boon in territory dominated by mosquitoes. All the good models on the market today have mosquito netting at the entrances and vents, and there are some tents made entirely of mosquito netting, very practical for hot mosquito country.

Though there is a wide range of designs to choose from, backpackers, because of the weight limitation, are pretty well restricted to the small, two-sleeper sizes, and these are offered in just two designs. There is the conventional pup tent, with the peak of equal height at both ends, and the mountaineer tent, which tapers from head to foot. Because there is less material and one pole is shorter than the other, the mountaineer design is usually lighter than the pup tent. Also, the taper offers a lower, more secure shelter in a windy camp.

A backpacking tent should have a waterproof floor, a vestibule or some other arrangement for extra space so you can store your gear without overcrowding, netting for the entry and vents, and a zippered door or tunnel.

Basically, you have a choice of three tent materials. Untreated, closely woven cotton, while heavy, has some real advantages over nylon tents. The fibers of the cotton swell when they get wet and thus provide a tight seal in a rainstorm. When the cotton dries, it opens up enough to breathe. Thus, under normal circumstances, you will not be troubled with condensation inside a cotton tent. A two-man cotton tent, however, weighs from seven and a half to ten pounds. There is a wide price range, though. While some are priced as high as sixty dollars, you can find others that are adequate for thirty dollars.

Untreated nylon, the second choice of material, seems to be the most popular, and I suppose the main reason is the light weight. Unlike cotton, however, its fibers do not swell up. Thus these tents must have a second roof or rain fly of treated nylon if you plan to camp in the rain. The untreated nylon is a good wind shelter, retains heat, and does not have condensation problems, but the necessity for a rain fly seems like nonsense to me. The rain flies themselves have their faults. If not rigged properly, they will flap against the tent, shedding condensation, or they will let wind-driven rain splatter the sides of your tent.

The untreated nylon tents must have a roof or fly of treated nylon to keep out the rain. This model is five feet wide and seven feet long, about minimum space for two campers and their gear. Courtesy Alpine Designs.

In addition, the treated nylon loses its waterproof character with time, and this means that you must replace the fly after a few seasons. The tent, fly, poles, and pegs, however, can weigh in at slightly more than five pounds—a real advantage. On the other hand, you cannot buy one of these tents for less than sixty dollars, and some go as high as a hundred fifty.

Your third choice of materials is treated or coated nylon. These are even lighter than the uncoated tents with flies, but the nylon with the waterproofing material closing the spaces between the weave makes for a tent with serious condensation problems. Designers have tried to cure the condensation problems with strategically located vents. The vents help, but they don't help enough. Water still collects inside the tent. You can live with it, I suppose, particularly if you are attracted by the four and a half pounds that these tents weigh. And you can buy a good one for about forty dollars, much more reasonable than a tent with a rain fly.

There is one other kind of tent not yet described. By definition, it falls somewhere between a tarp and a tent. This is the plastic tube tent, popular with many backpackers. To rig a tube tent, run a line through it, and tie the line between two trees or braced poles. Then weight the floor down with rocks or simply with your gear, and you have a peaked tent, open at both ends but still subject to condensation problems.

Tube tents evidently look enough like a real tent to make many campers believe that they are following tradition, but the things are really tarps with restricted versatility. You can buy a tube tent for less than four dollars, and it should last a season.

The catalogs offer kits with special poles and pegs for pitching a poncho as a shelter. You can make do with ingenuity in place of the special kit to rig your poncho as an emergency sleeping shelter. I know some campers in the Southwest who carry nothing more for shelter than a poncho. The models with grommets along the sides, of course, are easiest to rig, and some ponchos come with snaps that allow joining of two ponchos for a roomy shelter.

As you can see from the above, there is a wide choice of camp roofs, but no matter what you decide upon as best for your needs and style of camping, I hope that early in your outdoor ventures you make use of that finest roof of all—the star-studded sky. It's pretty hard to beat.

Chapter 5

CAMP COOKING

Keep It Simple

There has been so much written about camp cooking, about what you must do and what you must not do and about complex recipes for the open fire, that you may be shocked to discover that the subject is a simple one. At least, it should be kept simple for backpack camping.

You do not have to study nutrition and you do not have to count vitamins or calories to plan a camp menu. And as for the actual cooking, you will be surprised by what a healthy appetite can tolerate. Perhaps the rice is watery. Perhaps the eggs are slightly burned. After a day of hard hiking, both rice and eggs will taste delicious.

I suppose the main reason that many campers look upon cooking as some kind of mystery is that they rarely do any cooking around home. Perhaps they have never prepared a meal before in their lives. If this applies to you, please do some practice cooking at home before you go camping. Put some meals together, preferably with food you plan to use on your trip. Limit yourself to the utensils and pots you plan to carry. Your efforts, even if faulty at first, will eventually give you confidence, and who knows, your family may help you eat what you have prepared.

Just what foods should you take on a trip? The best test is palatability. Do you like it? Is it good enough to eat? Once the food you are considering passes this test, there are a few other conditions it must meet before you put it in your pack.

Weight, ease of preparation, packaging, cost, nutritional value, and volume all must be considered.

Weight, of course, becomes more important with the length of your trip. For an overnight outing you can carry a few items of canned food, but for long trips you must leave the canned goods at home. The only exception might be a can of meat, highly concentrated in protein, and you would open this the first day to reduce the weight of your pack as early as possible. Your major food supply, however, will be in the form of dried or dehydrated food. Outdoor suppliers have made tremendous advances in the past two decades in the preparation of dehydrated foods. About two pounds of the stuff will fill your needs for a day. There are basically two methods of preparation —vacuum dry, with the moisture sucked out by the heating oven, and the newer freeze dry, with the moisture taken from the food in the form of ice crystals.

Most of the dehydrated foods are easy to prepare. Some require nothing more than the addition of hot water and a few minutes of simmering. A few, however, are complicated. There is a dehydrated pork chop, for instance, that must be soaked in a special solution and pampered with a paper towel before it can be cooked. I am told it is delicious, but it sounds like too much fuss for a camper who carries just two pots and a pan. This brings up another point. Be leery of concoctions that require more than one pot. They can tie you up, leaving you nothing for boiling soup or tea water or for preparation of a side dish. Thus, before you pack dehydrated food, make sure you are equipped to handle it.

How the food is packaged is another important consideration. Cans and metal foil will not burn. You must take these things to the nearest garbage can. Given the choice between a burnable and a nonburnable package, other things being equal, take the burnable package. There are many items which you can repackage before your trip. We will go into detail on this later.

Cost must also be considered. Obviously, dehydrated food is more expensive than fresh or canned food, but usually the saving in weight is worth the extra money. There are, however, some "luxury" dishes that the budget-conscious camper can avoid, and there are many things on the grocery shelf, such as noodles, minute rice, dried peas, and dried potatoes, that make inexpensive but filling dishes.

Nutritional value is important. As we said, you do not have to be an expert, but you should know that food basically falls under three separate classifications. The carbohydrates, such as the starches and sugars, give quick energy. The proteins and the fats of meat products give a long-range reservoir of energy. Your camp menu should include all three types. Candy bars may give you quick trail energy, but if you eat nothing else, you may wake in the middle of the night, shivering and hungry.

Volume is yet another consideration in selecting food. Most catalogs offer food packaged for two, four, or six servings. In most cases, the estimate of what constitutes a serving seems to be on the conservative side. The fact is that you are extra hungry on a backpacking trip. A package advertised for four servings may well contain just the right amount for three. So don't skimp. In your menu planning, always figure on generous helpings. It is very unlikely that you will return from a trip with food left over.

So much for general considerations in buying backpacking food. Let's turn now to the details of the three main meals, plus that important supplement known as the trail snack.

BREAKFAST

Your first meal of the day should be a big one. This notion may be difficult to accept if your breakfast at home is usually a light one, but I urge that you eat heartily before beginning the day's labors. You may have to force yourself to eat a big breakfast that first morning in camp, but by the second day you should have no trouble eating. You will almost certainly wake up hungry.

Start with a hot drink. The instant powders make preparation of coffee or cocoa a simple thing. A tea bag, of course, is also convenient. I used to pack ground coffee and take great pride in my camp brews, but I succumbed to the convenience of instant coffee on about my fifth backpacking trip. With instant, there is no pot to clean out, no grounds to dispose of, and instant is really almost as good as fresh. Sugar in a hot drink gives quick energy. Powdered milk, particularly whole milk, provides fat for long-range energy. Powdered skimmed milk, while it dissolves easier than whole milk, is really more of a taste treat than an energy source.

Fruit drinks in powdered form are also convenient. You can simply add water to the powder and stir, but you will get better results by putting the mixture in a plastic water bottle and shaking it vigorously. I prefer Tang. It has a high sugar content, and one heaping teaspoon of the stuff makes a cup that tastes enough like orange juice to give your meal a touch of class. You can also buy powdered grapefruit and grape juice Tang.

Some campers swear by Jello mixtures served as a hot drink. It sounds like a high-energy, rib-sticking drink. One of these days I'm going to try it.

Dried fruit that is soaked overnight and stewed for breakfast makes another high-energy dish, and the fruit provides plenty of vitamins. Prunes, apples, pears, and apricots are all available in the grocery store in dried form. These are kiln or sun dried and carry more moisture than the dehydrated fruit available through outdoor suppliers. Thus, if weight is a serious consideration you will be better off paying a little extra for the dehydrated fruit. Some of the fruits, when stewed, become pretty tart, but you can cure this by stirring in a few spoons of sugar. The above fruits, plus raisins, dates, and dried figs, all make excellent trail snacks.

Cereals, either hot or cold, provide good energy food, at least most do. You should avoid the puffed or flaked cereals which are too bulky to be practical and often have low energy content. Brans make the best cold cereal, and the hot cereals, such as Malt-o-Meal, Cream of Wheat, and Wheatena are all good breakfast fare. My main objection to hot cereals, much as I like them, is that they leave a sticky mess in the pot. Granola, a favorite among many backpackers both as a breakfast food and a trail snack, is certainly nourishing food, but sample this stuff before you pack it. You may find, as I do, that you can eat very little before the taste and texture become monotonous.

The protein and fat in meat make it an excellent item to include in breakfast. Fresh bacon, because of the fat lost in frying, has to be considered a luxury for backpackers, but you can pour off the hot grease into a lidded tin for future use, particularly for use in frying trout, if you expect to catch them. Canadian bacon with low fat content is more practical, and outdoor suppliers sell concentrated bacon sticks that can be broken up and fried with other dishes. You can do the same thing with pemmican, the concentrated meat cakes that have served explorers and campers for years. The stuff is actually dried meat pounded up with melted fat and compressed into a cake. It can be used for the meat dish in any meal. Personally, I like it best fried with flaked mashed potatoes as a hash. I have often eaten this as the main course for breakfast.

Fish are best cooked as soon as possible after you catch them. If you are an early morning fisherman, and if you are lucky, you can include fish on the breakfast menu.

Eggs can be packed in fresh or in powdered form. Suppliers

sell special containers for fresh eggs, designed to prevent break-age. However, the stout cardboard and foam boxes used to package market eggs give excellent protection provided you use reasonable care to avoid crushing when you stow the eggs in your pack.

Powdered eggs have progressed far since World War II. Once awful, powdered eggs can now be rated good to excellent. One outdoor supplier offers powdered eggs with imitation bacon bits. You can scramble the mixture or try cooking an omelet. Either way, it is tasty.

Many campers have the idea that it is not a real camping trip until they start cooking pancakes. The batter is easily mixed with the dry pancake flour, but the syrup, which convention demands, can be a bother. Whole syrup is heavy to pack, so you will probably want to use the powdered syrups available from outdoor suppliers. These, of course, have to be mixed in a separate pot. If you are not fussy, a sprinkle of sugar and some melted margarine on a pancake may satisfy the syrup hunger. It is certainly more convenient. If you plan to cook pancakes, remember to include a spatula among your utensils.

Now don't get the idea from the above that you will in-clude all these things in one breakfast, but you will want variety. I always have coffee and Tang, but one morning the main dish may be scrambled eggs. The next morning it may be potato-pemmican hash. And the next it may be hot cereal and fish. Fish, by the way, are not too filling. Unless you are hauling in big lake trout, you will want some kind of rib-sticking supplement, like hot cereal. I used to have some kind of stewed fruit at each breakfast, but my habits have changed. I find it is more convenient to eat the fruit dry as a trail snack.

TRAIL SNACKS

After breakfast, this will most likely be the next thing you will eat. What you use for trail food is a highly personal thing.

Only you know what you like and how much you need. Thus each camper should be responsible for his own snacks.

Between-meal eating, frowned on by mothers and other nutrition experts, has a definite place in backpacking. You need several quick shots of energy during the hiking day. In your normal home life you may never touch anything between meals, and you may be one of those rare hikers who needs nothing on the trail, but don't count on it. Include candy or dried fruit as a personal item in your pack.

There are a great many sources of quick energy, too many to list here. It is perhaps best to start by saying what to avoid.

Highly salted nuts, crackers, or other foods will make you thirsty and perhaps lead you to drink too much water on the trail. Too much water can slow you down, even give you cramps. So avoid the salty stuff. Use salt tablets to supply your body's salt needs.

Avoid candies with low melting points, and avoid crackers that crumble easily. If you use greasy or sticky stuff, such as meat bars or fruit bars that may last through the day, use a plastic bag to protect your pocket or pack.

Obviously you will want to avoid excessive use of anything. Be particularly cautious of the artificial flavoring in some of the candy drops. Too much of this will pucker your mouth and make anything else you eat for the rest of the day taste like cotton. In fact, it is a good rule to avoid snacks with strong or unusual flavors. You can tire of them quickly.

So what is good? We have already mentioned dried fruit, pemmican, and fruit bars. For candy, I prefer a simple, no-nonsense bar of chocolate, but you may want something with a cream or coconut filling.

Gorp is a favorite of many campers, and you can mix this up to suit your taste. The common mixture calls for equal portions of peanuts, raisins, and chocolate bits. The M & M brand is an ideal gorp candy. Some mix in granola or another kind of bran cereal with their gorp.

Many of the catalogs list special trail food—everything ranging from sourdough cookies to lemon drops. One of the best things you can buy is the Kendal Mint Cake, an old standby for campers and mountain climbers. I carry two as emergency rations through most of a trip, but get to them in the final days for snacking. One six-ounce bar of mint cake packs six hundred calories.

LUNCH

You may eat trail snacks as frequently as once an hour, but don't let your snacking become a substitute for lunch. A real meal with some time to digest it will revive weary muscles—not to mention spirits. I prefer something hot, either a hot drink, such as tea or cocoa, or a thick soup. You can find dried soups on the grocery shelves which make excellent fare for camp lunches. There is a wide selection. The cream of potato and the mushroom are my favorites. Many campers consider cooking at noon a big bother, but it is surprising how these campers will change their views after you serve them a midday cup of soup. Incidentally, you should avoid the soups advertised for dieters. As outdoor food, they are weak and bland.

Sandwiches are difficult to make without bread. I know one family that packs bread despite the bulk, but the loaf is always gone by the second day. In other words, the family eats it up before the bread turns stale. In lieu of bread, you can make sandwiches with hard crackers such as Ry-Crisp or ship biscuits. Jams, jellies, and peanut butter can be packed in lidded tins or purchased in tubes from outdoor suppliers. The restaurant packs for table servings of jams and jellies are light and handy. Brick cheeses, though heavy, make nourishing lunch food, either with crackers or eaten alone.

There are many meats to choose from. Jerky is a hiker's standby. This dried meat will keep indefinitely if it is not allowed to get moist. A salami sausage also keeps well. Liver sausage, my favorite spread for crackers, and bologna do not keep so well in hot weather.

The catalogs list dehydrated luncheon delicacies such as

cottage cheese and chicken salad. If your taste runs to such things, by all means try them.

DINNER

Most of the foods mentioned so far can be purchased in your grocery store. For dinners you will probably rely more heavily on the dehydrated offerings of the outdoor suppliers. I think the main reason for this is convenience.

After a long day of hiking you just will not feel up to a great deal of fussing around your cooking fire. At the same time, you will be hungry, perhaps extremely hungry. A main dish that can be prepared simply by adding hot water, stirring, and simmering will be a godsend. I am partial to the beef and chicken stews and chili beans offered by Mountain House. A package of any of these dishes that serves two costs about two dollars. For a few cents more you can buy shrimp creole, which is excellent. All these freeze-dried preparations have good flavor, and for normal tastes they need no additional seasoning. I give these foods a few more minutes of soaking and a few more minutes of simmering than the directions suggest.

The only fault, as I have already mentioned, is that the servings seem a little skimpy for a hungry hiker. You will probably want a side dish. Rice, powdered potatoes, and dried peas all work well as stomach fillers. I often make up a large batch of mashed potatoes and save what is left over for potato hash at breakfast. Sometimes I add a few more dried flakes to stiffen the mixture for frying.

Of course, you do not have to have dehydrated food on the dinner menu. Spaghetti with powdered sauce preparations, noodles and cheese, and mashed potato flakes can be purchased in your grocery store. You can make any of these dishes more interesting and nourishing with gravies that can be purchased as powders packaged in envelopes at most groceries. Potatoes, beef gravy, and a few chunks of pemmican all mixed together

in a gooey mess is one of my favorites. For variety, I sometimes substitute rice or noodles for the potatoes.

A hot drink such as tea, coffee, or cocoa is good for starting
or capping off the evening meal. When I'm tired, I like a cup
of tea soon after reaching camp. It helps me relax and forget
about my tired limbs.

If you like desserts, you might want to try ice cream. It is
one of the unusual delicacies offered in freeze-dried form.
You eat it dry, by the way. Dried fruit, cookies, or simply a
candy bar will also satisfy your sweet tooth. If you have spent
the day in camp, you can even have Jello. Its main drawback
is that it ties up a pot all day because you have to cool it at the
edge of a stream or lake for several hours to make it gel.

You can "bake" cornbread, gingerbread, or biscuits, using
sticks of dough offered by outdoor suppliers. You place the
dough in a covered frying pan over a low fire. Enough dough
to serve four campers costs about sixty cents.

STAPLES

Though needs and tastes vary, you should figure on an
ounce of sugar, ⅛ ounce of salt, ½ ounce of margarine, and
½ ounce of powdered milk, as a cream substitute, per person
per day. You will also want to include pepper, perhaps some
curry powder, and other special herbs. Individual menus may
call for an increase in some of the basics. Flaked potatoes,
for instance, need milk for conversion to mashed potatoes. And
if you plan on frying many dishes you will need extra margarine. Buy margarine that is packaged in plastic cups rather than
in cubes.

Even if you use little sugar at home, you may develop a
sweet tooth when camping. This is the body's way of showing
its demand for extra quick-energy fuel. Thus beginners will
be wise to pack generous portions of the staples for the first
trips. With experience, you will be able to judge your needs
more accurately.

We have already mentioned salt tablets. They come close to being a necessity for all trips and are certainly necessary for hot-weather hiking. The reason is that you cannot supply your working body with all the salt it needs at meals without making your food unpalatable.

There may be other staples you will discover you need after reading directions on food packages. Some of the gravies, for instance, call for a tablespoon of flour. That is why you should read all directions before you leave home.

Because grocery packages are often too flimsy, too bulky, too heavy, or else contain more food than you need, you will want to repackage food for your trip. The handiest things for this are the bags sold for home freezing made of .022-inch-thick plastic. They come in several sizes, ranging from a pint to a quart. You will make most use of the pint-size ones because you will usually be packaging in portions to handle one meal at a time. For instance, if you plan noodles for Wednesday and again on Friday, you will pack two premeasured packages with enough in each to serve all in your party.

Since many items look alike in the clear bags—sugar and salt even feel much the same—you must label most bags to save time and prevent confusion. I have had poor luck with marker pens. Thus, I write "sugar," "salt," or whatever on both sides of a small piece of paper which I put inside the bag. If there are directions you might forget, copy them from the original package onto the piece of paper.

You can tie the bags by twisting the tops and using the paper-covered wires that are sold with the bags. Take care to fold back the ends of these wires so that they do not poke holes in neighboring bags. It is a good idea to package fine-grained stuff like sugar and flour in two bags, one inside the other, to reduce the chance of leakage.

When you empty a bag, you can burn it in a hot fire. In addition to the freezer bags, you will also need larger bags of tougher plastic that are sold as trash-bin liners. These help you keep breakfast, lunch, and dinner items sorted out and save a good deal of searching and digging through your pack. You will also want separate bags for trail snacks, staples, and perhaps first aid items. And you will want to carry a bag to pack up the garbage that you must carry out. Fortunately these liner bags come in many different colors, which will help you find things in a hurry without the bother of labeling.

For special packaging problems, particularly greasy or sticky things, you can buy light, lidded tins from outdoor suppliers, or you can collect empty baking-powder tins and similar containers. These tins, particularly if they contain bacon grease or margarine, which have a way of leaking through the tightest seals in hot weather, should be carried inside plastic bags to protect other gear in your pack.

Of course there are some grocery packages, such as envelopes of dry soup or gravy, that need no repackaging. Also, there is rarely any need to repackage the dehydrated food you buy from outdoor suppliers. It is usually hermetically sealed in light, tough packages which protect the food better than any package you might devise.

COOKING UTENSILS

Though iron pots and pans make excellent cooking gear, they are simply too heavy for backpackers. Aluminum, though it does not distribute heat as evenly as iron, makes up for this lack in light weight. A set of nesting aluminum pots with a pan that can serve either as a lid or a frying pan makes an ideal setup. Several models and types are available from outdoor suppliers. My kit, which has two pots and a pan plus vicegrip handle, costs about five dollars.

Beginning campers who want to defer this expense can make perfectly serviceable pots out of coffee cans or other cans of similar capacity. You can punch two holes near the top on opposite sides of the can and bend in a wire bail, or

For cooking convenience, it is hard to beat this kitchen of aluminum nesting pots and a gas stove that fits into a package less than five inches high. Author's photo.

Taken apart, the kitchen becomes a combination lid-frying pan, two pots, a wind screen, and a pair of pot vice grips, all made by Sigg, and a stove, made by Svea. The funnel was purchased separately. If you have a steady hand you will not need it for pouring fuel. This kit weighs less than two and a half pounds. Author's photo.

you can carry a pair of pliers to handle your hot pots. Add to this a light frying pan and you will be in business.

What are your minimum cooking needs? You can get by with two pots, a small one with two- to three-pint capacity and another one about a pint larger. A frying pan with about a six-inch diameter is adequate for two campers. One that is teflon-coated cleans easily, but you must use a wooden or plastic spatula with these to avoid scratching the coating.

Close-up of the Svea stove shows its simple design. Heat from the burner forces the white gas in the container to expand and rise through the stove neck. The valve with a detachable handle controls the flow. The heat of your hands is enough to generate the flow and get the stove started. The Svea, just one of several good models on the market, will start a quart of water boiling in less than seven minutes. It weighs one pound two ounces. Author's photo.

An aluminum bottle with a leak-proof cap makes the safest container for fuel. It is a good practice, however, even with leak-proof bottles, to store them upright in your pack. Author's photo.

In action, the Svea-Sigg combination is clean, quick, and efficient, a great convenience for an early morning start and for a hot lunch on the trail. You can defer the expense of this kit by using wood fires, but a gas stove, once you do acquire one, is liable to spoil you. Author's photo.

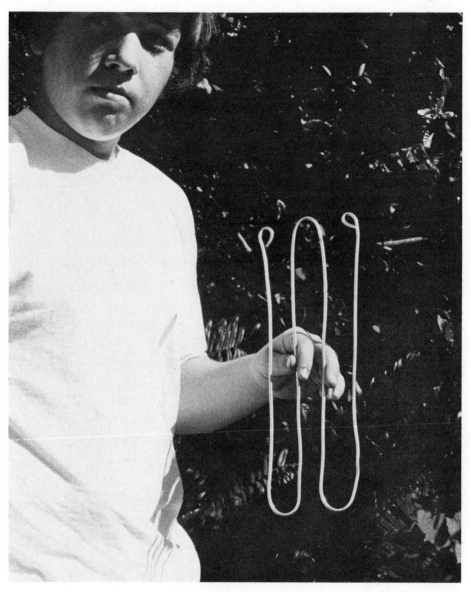

Six feet of No. 9 wire, a pair of pliers, and a little muscle are all it takes to make a grill. The ends are bent into loops to prevent the grill from poking holes in neighboring items in the pack. The grill should be stored in a stout cloth or plastic bag because it will become sooty with use. Author's photo.

The dingle stick and the gallows are traditional in the art of woodcraft. Remember to use green limbs and make sure that the structures are solidly anchored.

The ideal cooking fire should be small. Heat and smoke from a large fire will make cooking uncomfortable at best. This cook keeps his plastic water bottles and his cup within easy reach. Author's photo.

The minimum eating gear for each individual is one spoon, preferably a little larger than a teaspoon, a pocket knife, and a large cup. Cups that are chemically coated, such as the Sierra Cup, hold heat longer and will not blister your lips when you try to sip hot drinks. What about forks and plates? You don't need them. The aluminum plates sold with some cooking kits make fine pot lids, but they disperse heat so rapidly that a hot meal will often be cold before you can finish it.

What else must you have? Hot pads work for handling pots over a fire, but I prefer pliers or vice-grips. You will need a spatula if your menu includes omelets or pancakes, and if you pack any canned goods, you will need a can opener. The small, GI opener sold in surplus stores is ideal for backpacking.

I carry a homemade grill of No. 8 wire bent in the shape of a tall W. The catalogs offer stainless steel grills with stout cloth bags for packing at $6.25.

If your pots have bails, you can hang them over your fire with a dingle stick or a gallows, but I prefer to build a fire between two flat stones that can be bridged by a grill. Remember, if you use sticks, they must be green.

Since pots and grills collect soot, you must pack them in stout plastic or cloth bags to protect other gear in your pack. Don't spend fruitless hours trying to scrub soot off pots. Actually, the soot improves a pot's heating efficiency. At least, that is the claim of old-timers.

Of course, you will want to clean up the inside of your pots and your individual eating gear thoroughly after each meal. Each camper should be responsible for his own cup, spoon, knife, and whatever else he chooses to use. It is best to have the cook clean the pots and pans, and with a minimum collection of pots and pans it is usually a simple chore. A little hot water helps in soaking for the tough jobs, and river or lakeshore sand makes excellent scouring material. Take care, however, not to spill waste food at the water's edge. Scrape out as much as you can and dump it on the fire while the fire is still hot enough to burn it. Then scour out the stubborn residue. If you use soap, work on the pots in camp, not at the water's edge, and dump the water on dry ground, well away from the fresh water. Fastidious campers carry steel or fiber scouring pads. They are kinder to the hands than sand and certainly easy to pack. Try both and decide what you prefer. Use whatever makes the job easiest. Actually, if you take pride in your gear, you'll find that cleaning up is not much of a chore. It can be fun.

Chapter 6

YOUR PACK

What's Best?

No single thing has revolutionized backpacking as much as the introduction hardly twenty years ago of the contour backframe with hip belt. The backframe with a pack bag cut to fit has become such a common sight in some parks and forests that you might think there is no other kind of pack. This, however, is not the case.

There are a few hikers who will still argue that the backframe is not necessarily the best. I believe these few are even now dwindling in number, but the point is that as a beginner, you can start without making the big investment necessary for a quality backframe. There are more modestly priced alternatives which can serve you well, particularly for those first overnight trips. In fact, you may find that a large knapsack, a rucksack, or a packboard work so well for you that you will not want to make the change to a backframe. Before you decide on anything, however, you will want to know something of the traits, good and bad, of the various packs available.

The purpose of this chapter is to help you decide what's best for you.

THE KNAPSACK

If you have taken day hikes or picnics, perhaps you have already used a knapsack. It was probably a small one with room for your lunch, some extra clothing, and perhaps a camera. Knapsacks, however, come in a great range of designs and sizes. The big, rectangular knapsacks, known as Duluth bags in the Midwest, are almost bottomless and have room for enough gear for a trip of several days.

Essentially, no matter what the size or design, a knapsack is a pouch of canvas or tough nylon equipped with adjustable shoulder straps. Some have outside pockets on the sides, back, or in the top flap for extra, easy-access storage. Some have reinforced bottoms of leather or extra-thick cloth. And some have waist belts to hold the pack close to the body and to put some of the burden on the hips rather than entirely on the shoulders and spine.

One thing a knapsack lacks is a stiff frame of wood, wire, or light tubing either inside or outside of the pack. Thus, when you pack a knapsack you must be sure that soft items, such as spare clothing, folded tarps, or perhaps your sleeping bag, line the front side of the bag, which is the side that will be resting against your back.

A large knapsack, as we noted above, has tremendous capacity, but a heavy knapsack puts great weight on your shoulders. The load forces you to lean forward so that some of the weight shifts to the spine and hips. This is an uncomfortable and tiring way to walk.

Is there a maximum load for a knapsack? The answer depends on the strength and stature of each individual. My

A well-designed knapsack serves well for overnight trips and even for trips of several nights if you can pack sparingly. This bag is eighteen inches high, fifteen inches wide, and nine inches deep. It has padded shoulder straps and is rigged with exterior straps and buckles for outside gear. Courtesy Camp Trails.

limit is about twenty pounds, but there are campers who tote thirty-five pounds and more in knapsacks.

Your knapsack should measure about twenty inches high, sixteen inches wide, and six inches deep. You cannot expect to find one this size for less than fifteen dollars. A small pack can serve, but you will have to tie bulky items like sleeping bags and foam pads on the outside, a practice never very satisfactory with a frameless pack.

THE RUCKSACK

The term "rucksack" covers a variety of packs, but all are distinguished from a knapsack by having an external or internal frame. Most of the internal frames are pliant, allowing you to make adjustments to fit the load to your back. The external frames, usually of light tubing rigged with webbed slings over the hips or back, are an advantage in hot-weather hiking because the frame allows air to circulate between you and your load. This reduces sweating, which can be an annoyance with a knapsack or internal-frame rucksack.

A rucksack with interior aluminum frame is a favorite of skiers and mountain climbers because it can carry hefty loads with a low center of gravity. Many backpackers also find them completely adequate. This model has an unpadded waist belt. Courtesy Alpine Designs.

The rucksack frame also protects you from sharp objects within the pack. You do not have to load it with as much care as you do a knapsack.

I have known hikers who can carry up to fifty pounds in a rucksack without complaint. Forty pounds was my limit, but I was using one of the Bergen types, purchased from an army surplus store soon after World War II. This rucksack, developed in Norway, was adopted for U.S. mountain troops, mainly, I suppose, for its low center of gravity and high carrying capacity. Its external yoke frame with webbed sling was designed to ride on the hips. However, the pull of the load on the shoulder straps was so strong that it forced you to lean far forward. This brought the sling up over the tender kidney zone. I said I carried forty pounds in one of these but, as you can guess, it was not without complaint. However, a modern rucksack is far better than the old Bergen.

Rucksacks vary from the small models for children up to adult packs twenty-four inches high, seventeen inches wide, and seven inches deep. Most have outside pockets. The large models cost twenty-five to thirty dollars apiece.

THE PACKBOARD

The packboard, with tightly stretched canvas or nylon lashed between vertical members of the frame, was at one time the best piece of packing gear on the market. Indeed, many old-timers still consider it tops. The canvas or nylon serves as a sling to cushion the load against your back and allow air circulation.

In some regions of the Northwest the Alaskan packboard or Trapper Nelson remains a common sight. This has a wooden frame with a detachable bag. You can also find frames made of tough plastic (army-type) and frames made of aluminum. The "official" Boy Scout frame has tube uprights and cross members of wide bands, all light aluminum. Many manufacturers offer three sizes, with prices from about eight dollars up.

Packboard advocates claim that it holds loads closer to the body than other packs, thus putting the main carrying effort directly on the hips and legs rather than on the shoulders and spine, and the advocates like to tell about the veterans who have carried 120 pounds over miles of mountain trail. Sometimes the stories run to 130-pound loads and more. Actually, I believe many of these stories. Let's face it, the old boys were tough.

One of my earliest packs was a dufflebag lashed to a wood-frame board. I carried sixty pounds with the rig, but that was thirty years ago. I would not try that today with any pack.

However, the packboard might be right for you, particularly if you have a tight budget. But remember, it is essentially a flat slab resting against a curved back, and no matter what the advocates claim, your shoulders and spine carry much of the load. It takes conditioning and something of a stoic nature to use a packboard. I recommend that you start with light loads, say twenty to twenty-five pounds. Later, you can increase the weight, and who knows?—you may become an old-timer who swears by packboard camping.

Many packboards, and this is true of many knapsacks and rucksacks as well, have unpadded shoulder straps. You can make shoulder-strap pads with rectangular pieces of ensolite about ten inches long and cut about an inch and a half wider than the strap, allowing three-quarters-of-an-inch overlap on each side. Cut slits to take the strap about an inch and a half from each end. Slide the strap through the slits and position the pad so that it will ride on your shoulders. Use bands of ripstop tape to hold the pad in place. By covering the entire pad with tape, you will prolong its life. The pads will prolong your life, too, particularly if you hoist 120 pounds with your packboard.

THE CONTOUR FRAME

A host of modern campers owe a great debt to the packboard. It led to the development of the contour frame.

This frame, made of light aluminum or magnesium-alloy tubing, has a curve in the vertical members that follows the natural curve of your back. Tough, open-weave nylon webbing stretched between the uprights protects the back, and a variety of detachable bags offer the camper a marvelous selection of pack types and systems. Almost all bags on the market today are made of waterproof nylon. Padded shoulder straps with slide buckles for quick adjustment hold the frame close to the body, but the most important strap of all is the padded waist belt. The waist belt, buckled tightly—and it must be tight to be effective—brings the lower webbing of the pack hard against the hips. This puts most of the pack weight onto the hips and legs, leaving the spine relatively free of load.

Imagine the vertical members of a contour frame as a substitute spine connected to the hips by means of the waist belt. This explains why you can walk erect with a contour frame, even when carrying a heavy load, and it explains why hikers with bad backs can enjoy backpacking.

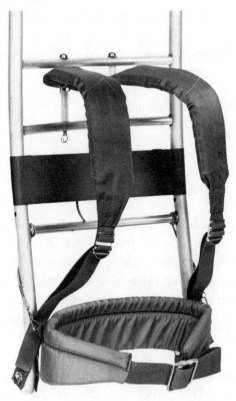

This sturdy contour frame can be adjusted through six different sizes to accommodate the growing hiker. The crossbars can be raised to new positions between the uprights, and the position of the shoulder straps on their vertical tubes can be adjusted as well. The bare frame gives a clear picture of the basic structure typical of all backframes.
Courtesy Camp Trails.

Veteran camper Bill Merrill, who suffered a broken back twice during his thirty-six years as a ranger, hikes with a contour frame and swears by it. In mountain trips ranging from Mexico to Alaska, Merrill has packed healthy loads with very little discomfort.

Merrill's pack is a Kelty, made by Kelty Pack, Inc., the pioneer in the development of the contour backframe. The firm began making frames in 1951, and the merits of the new system were recognized at once. Kelty soon had many competitors. Today, the major manufacturers include Trailwise, Camp Trails, Gerry, Alpine Designs, Sierra Designs, Mountain Master (Denali Company), Jan Sport, and, of course, Kelty. The competition has brought innovations and improvements. Most ma-

jor firms offer a wide choice of bag styles as well as a good selection of frame sizes.

What is the right size for you? Here is a table you can use
as a guide.

Body Height	Frame Height
5'3" and under	27"
5'3" to 5'7"	29"
5'7" to 6'	31"
6' and over	32½"

This is actually a rather rough guide. You must consider
torso length as well as body height. A long-legged six-footer
with a short torso might be happier with a twenty-nine-inch
pack rather than the recommended thirty-one-inch model. In
addition, individual manufacturers have different measures
for their standard sizes, but all the major firms offer at least
three, and often four, sizes that come close to the various
measures listed above.

The best bet, of course, is to try various models for size
in an outdoor-supply store. This saves the trouble and expense of returning models that do not fit when you order them
through the mail.

Many manufacturers, recognizing that their future rests in
the hands, or rather on the backs, of young hikers, now offer
special frames that can be extended to accommodate growing bodies. Kelty and Camp Trails offer a frame that can be
enlarged through three different sizes.

It is very difficult to pick out a single brand of frame and
bag as the best. I have talked to many hikers with many
different packs, and invariably each thinks that his own pack
is the best for him. I know I feel that way about mine. It
is a Trailwise. I suspect, however, that if I had carried some
other brand over the past several seasons, I would be just as
enthusiastic about it. The point is that it is the system—a
light, contour frame with a waist belt—rather than the brand
name that prompts all the enthusiasm.

The major criticism, perhaps the only criticism one can make against the system, is expense. A quality frame and bag will cost forty dollars or more, and like any other piece of camping gear, it is very difficult to suggest anything second-rate.

There are bargain buys, however, including some of the recently introduced Japanese imports. One of these, the Alpine Pack, sells for twenty dollars. It has padded shoulder straps and a nylon bag, but it does not include a waist belt. So you must figure on spending another seven to eight dollars for a padded belt. Jan Sport offers two models for young campers, a small, twenty-five-inch frame at twenty dollars and a twenty-nine-inch frame at twenty-five dollars.

If you want to delay this investment or if you are not certain of the model you want or the size that is best, look into pack rental. For a three-day trip, you can rent a frame and bag for about $3.50.

What type of bag is best? The three-quarter-length bag is certainly the most popular today. It allows space, usually at the bottom of the frame, for light but bulky items such as your sleeping bag, foam pad, or clothing. With nearly all models, you can change this around so that the space is at the top. The bags have cord ties, pins, or bolts which allow you to remove them from the frame and put them back in a different position. Lowering the bag lowers the center of gravity, a good idea for hiking steep trails.

The full-length bag covers the entire frame. Hikers who use it say it gives all their gear full protection against wear and the weather. They have a good point. With your sleeping bag strapped to the bottom of the pack, even though it may be in a stuff bag, you do expose it to wear. When you put your pack down or simply sit for a brief rest without taking off your pack, it is the bag that rests on the rough ground, bearing all the pack weight. The three-quarter-length bag, however, compensates in convenience. You can get to your sleeping bag without digging through all the other gear in your pack. The stuff bag for your sleeping bag should be waterproof, and you can protect it from wear by wrapping it inside your foam pad. True, this makes a bulky package, but pads are easier to replace than sleeping bags.

Tightening a slide buckle on a shoulder strap just slightly can greatly improve the comfort of a load. Loosening the buckles reduces the difficulty of getting in and out of a heavy load. Author's photo.

The more outside pockets your bag has the better. These not only help in the complex art of packing and finding gear, but they are also very helpful in packing the many things you will need on the trail, such as trail snacks, cameras, maps, a compass, water bottle, and so on. As for the bag itself, you will have a choice between compartmented and non-

A typical three-quarter-length pack bag is usually attached to the frame to leave room for the sleeping bag at the bottom of the pack. The bag can be shifted, however, if you wish to lower the center of gravity for steep hiking. Courtesy Alpine Designs.

A heavy-duty, full-length bag with five outside pockets and a zippered lower compartment is ideal for extended trips. Notice the exterior straps and hooks for additional gear. Courtesy Camp Trails.

compartmented design. Some packs have a lower, zippered section which you can get into without opening the main cover of your pack. Other packs have baffles inside the main compartment. Many hikers find these helpful in keeping their gear sorted out, but many others look upon them as obstructions. The baffles do sometimes make it difficult to find a spot for bulky items. It comes down, once again, to personal preference. My bag is a three-quarter-length model with two outside pockets, a zippered lower compartment, and no interior baffles in the main compartment. I like it, but I do wish there were more outside pockets.

SPECIALTY PACKS

There are some packs which remain strictly regional. The packbasket, for instance, is a common sight in the Midwest, particularly among canoe campers, but it would be a rare sight indeed to see one of these baskets in the western mountains of North America. Campers who have used baskets praise them, and they are reasonably priced. In its catalog, Stow-A-Way Sports Industries offers four sizes, ranging in price from $10.75 to $14.

One of the most interesting recent developments in pack design is the CWD pack offered by the Gerry Division of the Colorado Outdoor Sports Corporation. CWD stands for "controlled weight distribution," and the pack consists of four horizontal compartments, each with its own zippered opening. The idea is that you pack heavy items in the top compartments and lighter, bulky items in the lower compartments. This keeps the load close to the body, reducing back pull on the shoulders. The packs are offered in four sizes, the two larger sizes being equipped with built-in frames like a rucksack. Because of the compartments, the packs cannot handle large, bulky items, but the CWD system is gaining popularity, particularly among skiers and mountain climbers who want to keep loads close to their backs and among backpackers who take short, weekend trips.

A duffel bag equipped with shoulder straps or a plain duffel bag lashed up in a pack harness makes a bottomless pack for hauling bulky items. A friend and I equipped his cabin one spring after the forest road had washed out, using duffel-bag packs. They were ideal for this particular job—short haul of big loads—but for long camping treks the duffel bag gives more pack than you need. In addition, searching for some vital item deep inside a duffel bag is inconvenient at best. A pack harness, by the way, is simply a set of shoulder straps with two belts attached. The belts serve to bind a duffel bag or whatever else the load might be.

There are many other specialty packs, including a light, nylon day pack that you can carry inside your regular pack and break out for carrying a lunch and spare clothing on a side trip from camp. There is also a belt pouch which can serve the same purpose. A belt pouch is also very handy for camera nuts, as it offers a convenient carrier for extra lenses, film, and filters.

HOW TO PACK

The general rule, at least the rule you hear the most, is that heavy gear should go near the top of the pack and the lighter stuff should go in the bottom. The idea is that getting the center of gravity high and close to the shoulders makes the pack ride better. Instead of pulling back on the shoulder straps, it rides vertically, with the weight on the hips. I do not like to argue with established rules, but after a great deal of experimentation I'm inclined to take exception to this one. I think what is important is that you get your heavy gear close to the front of the pack. This is the part of the pack that rides next to your back. If the heavy stuff is stowed this way, it does not seem to make much difference if it is high in the pack or low; at least, that has been my experience.

With a knapsack or with some rucksacks this system of packing is sometimes difficult because most heavy items are hard and have to be cushioned to protect your back. However, with a little care you can cushion these things and keep them close to the front as well. Actually, the high-weight rule, if carried to extremes, can be dangerous. A top-heavy pack will upset your balance and cause a fall.

Another rule is so obvious it hardly needs emphasis. You must organize your pack so that you can easily find what you want. A few frustrating searches for something vital that you must have in a hurry will make you a believer in this rule. This is where outside pockets come in handy. Your plastic water bottle with leak-proof cap can go in a side pocket, ready for a thirst-quenching pause on the trail. If you carry fuel for a stove, the fuel bottle can go in a pocket on the opposite side.

Other items for outside pockets might include your flashlight, particularly if you expect a late arrival in the next camp, your map and compass, matches, a light windbreaker, trail snacks, toilet paper, sun lotion, insect repellent, salt tablets, foot-repair material such as moleskin or bandaids, a snake bite kit, and perhaps a camera. If you do not have enough outer pockets for all this, you can place some inside the main compartment near the top of the pack, where they can be found quickly.

A hiker who organizes his pack well should be able to get to things quickly during the day's hike. Having to dig deep into the dark corners of your pack is a sign of poor planning. Try to organize so that you do not have to open the main compartment of your pack until you stop for lunch, and keep your lunch supplies near the top, where you can find them quickly.

Chapter 7

ON THE TRAIL

FIRST DAY

You are eager to start. When you leave the car, bus, or what-ever else has brought you into the mountains, chances are you will want to put as many miles as possible between you and civilization.

Take it easy!

There are so many good reasons for moderation on the first day of a backpack trip that we will give just a few of them here.

Obviously, the first day is a day of adjustment, not only physical adjustment, but mental as well. As a beginner, you are embarking on a brand-new experience. You will certainly be a little tense and nervous. Even veteran backpackers rec-ognize the need for adjustment.

Often tempers are short that first day. If you try to cover

too much ground at the beginning, you may find yourself in a bitter argument with your best friend. These arguments are almost always over some trifling thing, but they can spoil the rest of the trip. Take my word for it.

A great deal depends on the drive that brought you to the mountains. Curvy roads can upset stomachs. A stuffy bus can leave you fuzzy-headed. Sitting for hours in the same position can leave your muscles cramped. Travel, no matter how it is accomplished, is tiring. And, of course, if you have climbed several thousand feet in your drive, you can become light-headed, weak, and nauseated in thin air.

There are no hard and fast rules on altitude sickness. Some campers "feel the altitude" with a climb of three thousand feet. Others can climb seven thousand feet and have no trouble. On some trips you will not be bothered. On others, sometimes even at lower elevations, you will. The point is that you must give your body time to adjust. Hiking out ten miles with a heavy pack is not the way to do it.

Unless you have left home very early, the drive to the trailhead has probably used up several hours of daylight. Common sense thus dictates that the first day's march must be a short one.

Many experienced backpackers do no hiking at all the first day. They simply camp out of the car in a public camp or set up camp just a few yards off the road. For several years, we have been lucky enough to have the use of a friend's cabin as the starting point for long mountain hikes. The temptations to enjoy this hospitality for more than one night are great, but except for one trip when rain drummed on the cabin roof for two days, we have hit the trail the morning after our arrival.

Still another reason for first-day restraint, and a major one, is pace. It takes time to find your pace, and it is highly unlikely that you will find it that first day.

HOW FAST?

Each hiker has his own pace, a speed of walking that suits him best. And pace varies with terrain, your physical condition, and the weight of your pack. All this makes pace difficult to describe in generalities, but it is extremely important. The wrong pace will wear you out quickly. If you have ever hiked behind a crowd of poky walkers, you know that too slow a pace can be almost as tiring as one that is too fast.

One veteran camper has declared that finding your pace when hiking with a pack is much like learning to walk all over again, and that you must go through the learning process with the start of each season. Although the right pace is a highly individual matter, here are a few tips that might help you find yours.

On level ground, your legs should swing from the hips. On grades, the knees and ankles will come into play, but on moderate terrain your length of stride should be controlled mostly by hip action.

A stride that puts a slight tug to the muscles along the backs of your legs puts you at the peak of walking efficiency. If the tug is painful, shorten your stride. If the tug is noticeable but not painful, chances are you are hitting the right stride.

Let your arms swing freely. The arms are important. You will notice that the left arm swings out as the right leg swings out, and the right arm swings out with the left leg. This helps keep your balance, and you will notice that arm-leg motion is bound together strongly. Make a conscious effort to swing your arms faster. You will start walking faster without thinking about it. Walking with your hands in your pockets or with thumbs hooked under your shoulder straps will not help you find your pace.

Incidentally, blood sometimes causes the swinging hands to swell on a long hike. The swelling will go down with a few moments' rest, but it can be painful if you are wearing a tight finger ring. Remove the ring before starting your hike.

Some campers are naturally pigeon-toed, but for those with normal feet, it is most efficient to plant the boot in the direction of travel. This way, the ankle gives the best and safest pivot. In climbing, you will get better traction by pointing the toes outward. Whether climbing up- or downhill, you will reduce the chance of slipping by planting the entire surface of the boot on the ground at once. This will seem unnatural to many hikers at first, but climbing on the balls of the feet or coming down on the heels can cause some nasty spills.

Posture varies with each hiker. Some, when climbing, lean far forward to carry almost all the pack weight on their back and shoulders. Others stay almost erect on all grades. No matter what suits you best, your upper body should not lunge back and forth or pitch from side to side as you walk. Such motion will not only tire you quickly but it can also cause you to lose your balance. If you find yourself pitching or swaying, check your pack. The center of gravity may be too high.

The danger of running with a pack on your back is almost too obvious to mention, yet I have seen novice hikers race down hills with no thought for their own safety and the safety of others. One slip and a running hiker can twist an ankle, break a bone, or even kill himself. The rule on running is: don't.

Even a forced pace, well short of running, can be dangerous. If you are in the position where you have to cover a great distance in too short a time, stop and review your plans. The risk of speed is too great.

Rate of breathing provides another means for finding the right pace. If your breath becomes forced, your throat becomes raspy, or your chest begins to hurt you are moving too fast for conditions of the trail. Some hikers say that your rate of breathing should not restrict conversation. In other words, if you have to gasp to say something, you are walking too fast.

The lungs' demand for oxygen increases with increase in body effort. A heavy load, a steep climb, or a fast pace will make you puff. In high altitudes it will not take too much increase in body effort to start you puffing, particularly if you have just arrived in the mountains. You must avoid prolonged, unbroken periods of heavy breathing. Break them up with brief but frequent rests.

WHEN TO REST

Resting is actually part of your walking pace. Some hikers do it by the clock, taking a five-minute rest after each twenty-five minutes of walking, or a ten-minute rest after fifty minutes, or follow whatever other formula suits them. This may be fine on level ground, but on a mountain trail you will vary rest patterns according to terrain. And you will find that many short rests are better for you than one long one. Here's why.

Working muscles produce acids, particularly lactic acid. If lactic acid accumulates in the muscles, they will begin to weaken, ache, and eventually cramp. Given the chance, your body can dispose of these acids efficiently. Blood, with fresh oxygen, will break down the acid into harmless compounds which the body can eventually eliminate. The body's acid-disposal system can work only so fast. You can take in a limited amount of oxygen with each breath. A limited amount of blood can be circulated through your body with each beat of your heart. In any kind of heavy work or activity our muscles produce acids faster than the body's acid-disposal system can take care of them. We must rest to let the system catch up. Fortunately, the system catches up very quickly. Rarely does it take longer than a minute. Return to normal breathing and a slower pulse indicate that your body has the muscle-acid problem under control.

From the above, we can see that the major purpose of the trail rest can be served in a very short time, that a five-minute rest can be no more efficient than a one-minute rest. In fact, there are some good arguments against long rest stops. In shaded or windy spots, the sudden drop in temperature can cause muscles to cramp and joints to stiffen. Also, a heavy psychological weight can descend on hikers who rest too long in easy comfort. It is simply hard to get started again.

Of course, none of this tells you what kind of rest pattern

to adopt. Each body functions differently. You have to work out a pattern that fits your body's demands. On a steep climb you may be forced to come to a brief, standing stop every fifteen to twenty yards. On level ground you may be able to walk for an hour without stopping. Downhill, you may find, as I do, that your knees start crying for mercy in about five minutes. You will want to rest.

Whether you stop with your pack on or off depends mainly on the length of your rest. Hoisting the pack back onto your shoulders is an extra bit of effort that should be avoided for the brief stops. You can sit with the pack braced against the ground so that most of the weight is off of your shoulders, and with sloping ground or a convenient boulder, your pack can become a back rest. Before leaning against trees, check them carefully for pitch. It makes a sticky mess that is hard to remove. For long rests, shed your pack, walk around a bit and stretch your unencumbered limbs.

Trail snacks and the water bottle come into use during rest stops. It is also a good time to take a salt tablet.

LUNCH STOP

A leisurely stop for lunch in a pleasant spot can provide the happiest interlude of your camping day. You will have a feeling of accomplishment. You have put some hard miles behind you. You can take your ease without the nagging responsibilities of setting up camp or breaking camp. In a way, you are at drift between bases. And if you have a warm boulder at your back, soft grass cushioning your tired muscles, and the muted symphony of a nearby brook in your ears, you can stay in this drifting state for a scandalously long time.

Does it matter? In such a state it is hard to think that anything matters.

There are, however, some responsibilities. The lunch, for instance.

We have talked earlier about camp meals, but let me say here again that something hot at lunch, even just a cup of tea, has marvelous powers of restoration for both the body and the spirit.

You should take almost as much pains in selecting your lunch spot as you do in selecting a campsite. By all means, try to stop by fresh water. If it is a hot day you will want shade. If it is windy you will want shelter. And, of course, if it is raining you will want a place where you can hang a tarp or poncho quickly. Obviously, if there is a view you will want to take advantage of it.

In addition to eating, the lunch stop is an ideal time to sort through your pack and organize it for the evening. If your schedule indicates a late arrival, you would be smart to group together everything for the evening meal in one plastic bag or at least in one convenient place in your pack.

The lunch stop also is a good time to check your feet for damage. You may want to change into dry socks, rinse out the old ones, and hang them on the outside of your pack to dry.

You should get out your map and compass during the lunch stop, find your position, and identify landmarks. Get your fellow campers involved in this orientation study. It is a good exercise in safety, and it is fun.

How long should you stop for lunch? This depends heavily on your hiking schedule for the day. I try to arrange a schedule that allows at least an hour for lunch. If you are not pressed for time, there is nothing wrong with a two- or even a three-hour stop. They may be the most memorable hours of your trip. The day's hiking schedule, obviously, is determined by time and distance. If you plan to cover fifteen miles of mountain trail in one day, it may take eight hours of hiking. This means an early start.

WHEN YOU HIKE

At home, it may be your custom to stay up late, watching television or reading. Prepare to change your ways on a camping trip. Surprisingly, it will probably not be a difficult change.

You will be tired enough that first evening in camp to snuggle into your sleeping bag soon after the sun goes down. You will sleep soundly, but you will probably wake up before dawn. Don't be dismayed. This is just as it should be. Of course, if it is several hours before sunrise, roll over and go back to sleep, but if it is around five in the morning, and there is a full hiking day ahead of you, it is time to start the fire for breakfast.

Many novice campers are tempted, particularly on cold mornings, to stay in bed until the sun warms their sleeping bags. This is a waste of valuable time. You will need all the hours of sunlight available for travel, and the early morning hours when the air is still cool and you are fresh are the most efficient hours for hiking. You want to eat up, clean up, and pack up without delay.

I know one father who gets his family moving before dawn. He hears plenty of cranky comment, but no one complains on arrival at the next camp in early afternoon, with plenty of time for fishing, exploring, or relaxing in the sun.

A late start, with the sun halfway up the sky, even if your journey for the day is a short one, tends to depress spirits. The miles seem longer than they really are, and you will think you are weary. Actually, the weariness is probably closer to simple disappointment over the loss of the best hiking hours of the day.

Get an early start.

TRAIL HAZARDS

You will come upon large fallen trees that block the trail. Usually you can get over or around these obstacles with little delay. A trail so heavily overgrown with brush that you practically have to crawl to get through can be far more troublesome and cut time from your schedule. A washout can bring you to a full stop.

Of course, you do not plan on meeting these hazards, but anyone who has camped for many seasons has had to face them. If the trail has been washed out by flood, slide, or

avalanche, leave your pack and see if you can scout out a safe
—repeat *safe*—detour. If your new route calls for holding on
to the side of a mountain with fingers and toes, it is not safe.
You simply have to turn back.

Streams are a common hazard. By midsummer most mountain streams can be forded safely, but early in the season
strong currents and deep water make these streams treacherous.

To ford a stream, the first step is to make sure the spot you
have chosen is the best available. Some mountain trails seem
to lead right across the deepest pools in the neighborhood.
This may be all right for horses and pack animals, but it is
not the best spot for hikers. Scout about a bit. You may find
some natural stepping stones that will allow you to cross without wetting your feet. If you do have to get wet, however, remove your boots and socks. With deep water facing you, you
should also remove your trousers. Put the socks and your
trousers in the pack. Now lace your boots on over your bare
feet and get your pack on your shoulders. Do not fasten the
waist belt of your pack. If you fall, you will want to be able
to slip out of it quickly. Now walk across the stream carefully, making sure of your footing with each step.

On the other side, remove your boots and drain them. Put
on your dry trousers, then, after drying your feet, your dry
socks. Get back in your boots. They will dry out on the trail,
and your socks will protect you from blisters.

Where streams are deep and strong they should be viewed
with extreme caution. With experienced campers in your party,
you may be able to cross safely by lining. This involves getting a leader across with a line that those who follow can use
as a hand hold.

Colin Fletcher, the famous solo hiker, "swam" rivers on his
Grand Canyon trip by sprawling crosswise on his air mattress
and kicking with his feet.

I recommend avoiding lining and swimming for beginners
unless they are camping under the close supervision of experienced backpackers. On those first trips, avoid large streams
or pick a time of year when they are down to safe levels.

YOUR GROUP

In this chapter we have discussed hiking techniques and pace almost entirely as it relates to one individual—you, but you will not be alone. You must consider your pace and your methods as they relate to your group. This can be a problem, and the larger the group the bigger the problem can become.

In a group of six or more, you can usually count on one sleepy camper to delay your start. On the trail, there will almost certainly be a dawdler who keeps others waiting, and there might well be a speeder who vanishes around the first bend and is not seen again for the rest of the day. Six campers spread out over four miles of trail can hardly be regarded as a hiking unit, certainly not a safe unit.

That speeder can take the wrong fork in a trail or suffer a fall. No one may know about it for hours. You cannot leave the dawdler behind, but while he is not as likely to get into as much trouble as the speeder, he will wear short the tempers of those who stay with him.

All this is a good argument for smaller camping groups and for splitting trail groups into two or more units, each with a leader who has a clear understanding of the day's hiking plan. Of course, it is unlikely that persistent dawdlers or racers will be invited on that next trip, but don't give up too early on these hikers. Reason sometimes works.

The racer usually races to prove himself. He wants to say he reached camp first, and he wasn't even tired. Testing ability and proving self-reliance are legitimate phases of backpacking, so it is hard to fault the racer's motives. But you can explain that cooperation, safety, and companionship are also important phases of the sport—phases good campers do not neglect.

The dawdler presents a greater challenge. If a hiker's best pace is an unusually slow one, it is difficult to demand a change.

I once asked a dawdler why she thought she was so much slower than everyone else, and she said her pack was too heavy. I immediately helped her unload about ten pounds and then distributed it between two other hikers and myself. Her pack weight, I think, had nothing to do with her problem, but she kept up with us the rest of the day. She was shamed into it.

For brief trail stops, there is no reason for everyone in your party to come together, but for longer stops it is a good idea to join forces and discuss your progress. If there are any complaints, they can be aired along with your tired feet.

Chapter 8

IN CAMP

The Ideal Site

The ideal campsite would have plenty of level ground, an ample supply of fresh water, a bounty of dry wood, an absence of insects, and shelter from wind and sun if needed. As a bonus, throw in a spectacular view.

Ideal sites do exist, but they are rare. It is sometimes difficult, in fact, to find a site that will meet your simple needs for comfort. For beginners, it is all too easy to pick the wrong site.

The success or failure of a trip can hinge on your ability to choose a campsite. It pays to be fussy and spend a good deal of time on your decision; and please, don't expect to have any luck picking a camp in the dark. Plan your hiking day so that you have at least two hours of daylight for selection of a site and for setting up camp.

When you find a likely spot, don't start unpacking at once. Stroll about, stretch your limbs, and get the feel of the place. You will notice things you did not see on your first inspection. Maybe you will change your mind and decide to keep looking. Sometimes just a few steps will bring you to a better site. It is frustrating to find that better site after you have unpacked.

After some experience, you will develop an instinct for good campsites, but in the beginning you will probably have to concentrate on searching out the basic elements of a good site. Let's consider them separately.

LEVEL GROUND

You can camp without fresh water, provided you have toted enough water with you, and you can camp without firewood, provided you carry a stove and fuel, but you cannot camp without level ground for sleeping. It does not have to be absolutely level. In fact, some campers prefer a slight slope so that they can sleep with their heads slightly higher than their feet, but ground that drops more than four or five inches from head to feet presents serious hazards. You and your bag will slide downhill during the night. You will be forced to interrupt your sleep constantly as you crawl back again and again to your starting place.

If you do not get a good night's sleep, you have missed the main purpose in making camp.

How much level ground you'll need depends, of course, on the size of your party. It does not take much space for two or three campers to bed down, but you should never be so crowded that there is a danger of one camper being shoved off the level space into oblivion. If you have a tent, the entire tent floor should be on the level. Don't try to get away with one low corner. A sleeper can slide there and take the tent with him.

In addition to having it relatively level, a comfortable sleeping area should be free of rocks, branches, and insect colonies. You can clear away rocks, branches, and other lumpy obstacles with relative ease, but there is no use in trying to move an ant hill. If ants are in possession, look for other ground.

The level ground should be dry and have good drainage, but it should not be in the middle of a drainage channel. Ditching a site to carry off drainage encourages erosion. If you take care in your search, you will find a bed site that does not need ditching.

FRESH WATER

A mountain stream with no permanent human settlements along its banks will give you a safe supply of water. High mountain springs and lakes are also reliable, but in lower regions where there is evidence of civilization or simply of heavy recreational use, you must begin to suspect all water sources.

If you have any doubt about the purity of water, boil it or use purification tablets. Ten minutes of boiling will kill unfriendly bacteria. At high levels, where water boils at a lower temperature, stretch the time to fifteen minutes.

Many backpackers carry Halazone tablets. One tablet releases enough chlorine to disinfect a pint of water. The tablets give the water a strong smell and taste of chlorine. It is harmless, but you can dispel some of it by stirring the water vigorously and then letting it stand in an open container for about half an hour.

Except in desert regions, poisonous mineral springs are rare. However, if you find water ringed by crystal deposits or lacking in all forms of plant or animal life, leave it alone.

WOOD

In well-traveled regions and at popular campsites, you may have to range far to find firewood. We are talking about dead wood. Never cut living plants for your fire. This is destructive. In addition, green wood will not burn.

A healthy forest produces dead wood. Low branches,

shaded by those above, die and fall to the forest floor. This "squaw" wood can almost always be pounded into shorter sections with your boots. It makes ideal camp fuel. In addition, bark and branches of fallen trees, driftwood along stream or lake banks, even pine cones can fuel your fire. You do not need an ax or hatchet to gather wood. Branches that cannot be broken over your knee or with your boots are too big for a cooking fire.

During or after a rain, you may have trouble finding dry tinder to start a fire. Dry leaves, pine needles, or twigs can sometimes be found in the shelter beneath fallen trees. Also, you can use your knife to split finger-size twigs and shave the dry, inner wood into tinder. In addition, you can save paper from food wrappers during the day and store it in a dry pocket for starting your fire.

Many campers currently argue against wood fires, saying that taking the dead wood destroys natural life cycles in the forest. Grubs, wood worms, and other boring insects live in the wood, and these provide food for other animals such as rodents and birds. These same campers also object to the charcoal and ash deposits of dead fires. Instead of cooking on wood fires, they carry camp stoves, usually the type that burn white gas.

On the other side of the argument, wood burners claim that clearing dead wood reduces the fire hazard and helps cut down the population of destructive insects.

You will undoubtedly take sides in this debate. Perhaps you have strong feelings already. Personally, I must confess that my own practices are ruled by practical convenience. For a quick start in the morning, nothing can match a gas stove. For a leisurely evening, I like a wood fire. Of course, in the desert or above the treeline you will need a stove, but for beginning campers, anxious to hold expenses down, a stove is one of the purchases you can delay.

INSECTS

We have discussed the insect problem in an earlier chapter, but we must consider it again in camp selection. Swamps, ponds, lakes, any body of still water, can manufacture mosquitoes. If you camp near still water, try to pick high ground that is exposed to wind for your site. Avoid setting up camp amid thick, low-lying brush. This brush can shelter mosquitoes and other pesky insects.

Never argue with insect colonies over the right to a campsite. Beehives, like ant hills, are difficult to move. Do not scatter food that will attract insects. Yellow jackets are fond of raw meat. Ants will swarm over spilled sugar.

Fire smoke will discourage mosquitoes. In fact, early in the evening, you might be fooled into thinking there is no problem, but when your fire dies and you are settling down to sleep, the mosquitoes start their attack. Have some repellent within easy reach when you go to bed.

SHELTER

Wind can turn an ideal camp into a miserable one, sometimes suddenly. If a sudden wind comes up after you have set up your camp, the temptation is to hold on and tough it out. Usually, you would be better off moving at once to sheltered ground. In the mountains, the down-canyon winds of the evening can scatter fire cinders, flatten tents, and carry off light gear. Your best defense is to find a site behind a cliff or rock face or a thick grove of trees that will give reasonably calm air.

In a light rain you can find temporary shelter under trees, but camping under trees in a rain gives little benefit. The trees, in fact, will continue to drip and the ground beneath will remain damp long after a rain has stopped. Trees in a snowfall can be downright treacherous, bombing you with globs of the cold, soggy stuff. Usually your best shelter against rain or snow is your tent or tarp pitched on well-drained ground.

Old trees with many dead branches are dangerous, even in good weather. Don't camp under them, and in a high wind stay well clear of them.

In some regions there are large caves which offer good shelter from rain and wind. Personally, caves make me nervous, but if they don't bother you, use them. Camp near the mouth of the cave so that your fire smoke does not suffocate you and you have plenty of light. Remember, in a lightning storm the mouth of a cave or overhanging cliff can be extremely dangerous.

CAMP PROCEDURES

Once you have selected a campsite, what do you do next? This depends on circumstances. If it is raining, you will want to set up your tarp or tent at once. If the weather is clear but the day is growing late, the first step will probably be to gather wood and get the fire started. If it is midafternoon and there is no pressure, I like to spend a happy half hour doing nothing. On a hot day nothing feels as refreshing as a dip in a mountain pool.

But back to setting up camp. Usually, after making sure there is good, level ground for a bed, I give first attention to the fire. If there is already a fire pit left by previous campers, use it. It is silly to dot a good site with several heaps of ashes and blackened rocks. I build a fire in a miniature canyon between flat rocks. When no rocks are available, it is possible to dig a trench. Your light grill can bridge the rocks or lips of the trench to hold the cooking pots.

Do not locate your fire against tree roots, and be sure to clear away pine needles, leaves, dry grass, or anything else that might burn, for a radius of five feet or more from the fire. If it's a windy day, make this ten feet.

You do not need a big fire for cooking. A big fire is not only dangerous, but it will also drive you away from your pots and make cooking hot, difficult work.

There has been much detail written on how to start a fire. The basic necessities are heat, dry tinder, and air, and the tendency among most novice campers is to neglect air. The air carries oxygen. Without oxygen, even the best tinder will not burn. So stack your dry leaves, pine needles, wood shavings, or whatever you happen to be using in an open pattern so air can circulate. After you have touched a match to the tinder, add twigs or split branches gradually, never allowing their weight to crush out the flames.

After the fire is well started, burning branches that are an inch or so in diameter, you can put on a pot of water and turn for the moment to other duties. I go to the bed site, spread the ground cover, roll out the mat, and shake out the sleeping bag. If you have a down bag, you should pat it out vigorously to distribute and loft the down.

Next, after checking the fire and restoking it, if necessary, you can rig your tarp. Of course, if you have a tent, that goes up before you break out your mat and sleeping bag.

After the sleeping area is in order you can turn to your pack, putting things you may need during the night, such as a flashlight and insect dope, next to the bed, and carrying things for the evening meal to the fire. By this time your water should be hot if not boiling, and you can turn your attention to the evening meal.

SANITATION

This portion of camp procedure is so important that we will give it a separate section. Many don't like to talk about sanitation, evidently with the notion that if you don't talk about it the problem will go away. The fact is, drawn from the evidence of despoiled camps I have seen, we do not talk about it enough.

Let's face it—every healthy body must get rid of wastes.

You must eliminate your wastes in a manner that causes as little offense and danger to others as possible.

Go well away from camp. Choose a spot that is not near a waterway, even a dry one. Use your boot to scuff a cat hole several inches deep in the soil. Use this hole and when you are through, bury both your feces and the toilet paper with loose soil.

Burial not only hides the unsightliness of your deposit, but it also discourages flies. Flies spread dysentery and other bacterial diseases that stem from human waste. Some campers carry a light trowel for sanitation. It is handy but not necessary.

In an improved camp, use the public toilets.

When finished with elimination, wash your hands with soap and water as soon as you return to camp. This is a further guard against disease.

Regarding soap, the general rule is to use it sparingly, and not to take it to the stream or lake and make suds. Wash hands, clothes, or dishes in camp when you use soap, and dump the waste water on dry ground, well away from the camp's water supply. Do not take detergents containing phosphates on your camping trip. Phosphates promote the growth of green scum, stuff that can choke out other water life.

Garbage, another sanitation problem, would not be a problem if everyone followed this rule: if it won't burn, carry it out. Tin cans, foil wrappers, and aluminum trays will not burn. You carried this stuff into the wilderness. It is a simple thing to carry it out. Burying nonburnables does not work. Animals dig the things up because of the food scent.

Wet garbage, such as unused noodles or mashed potatoes, will burn in a hot fire, but do not expect success when the fire is almost out. What about leaving such garbage for the animals? This, as we have already explained, is no favor to the animals, and it can be disastrous to you if your offering attracts thieving animals. This leads to another step in camp procedure.

THE FOOD CACHE

It is handy when using a stove and when camping with a small group to cook breakfast in bed. You have all the materials at hand when you turn in at night. Then, in the morning, working from the warmth of your sleeping bag, you can start the stove, heat the water for tea or coffee, and mix up your powdered eggs or cereal or whatever else happens to be on the menu.

If you are not in semitame bear country and your camp is not surrounded by chipmunks, you can usually get away with keeping the breakfast food beside your bed. Animals will not escape with much food if you are a light sleeper and have a flashlight handy, but some of the gnawing beasts can do extensive damage to packs, trying to get to your food. Keep it in a plastic bag, and if there are animals about, you will have an easier sleep if you store the breakfast food in the cache with the rest of your edible supplies.

An unused stuff bag that is waterproof or a large plastic bag make good caches. Tie the opening closed tightly with your longest line. Coil the other end of the line and throw it over a limb. Then hoist the cache aloft and secure the line to the tree trunk. The cache should hang freely, well away from the trunk of the tree. Sometimes you cannot find a handy limb. You can rig a line between two trees, tie the cache in the middle, and lift it by tightening the line.

What about camps without trees? There are situations where you cannot cache your food. You simply have to sleep next to it and be prepared to defend it.

BREAKING CAMP

The most important thing in breaking camp is the fire. Make sure it is out. As soon as you have finished the final meal, pour water on the coals and spread them out. Then go about the business of dismantling your tarp or tent and packing your gear. Then pour more water on the fire until every hiss of every cinder is silenced. Stamp on the coals and pour on more water. Then do your final packing chores before checking the fire again. It should be cold to the touch.

The point of this prolonged procedure is that it takes time to make sure a fire is really out. One hot coal can be blown to life by a wind. You do not want to have a forest fire on your conscience.

Perhaps the most frustrating thing about breaking camp is forgetting something. If it is something vital, you will have to come back for it. This can mean a hike of several miles.

Check camp thoroughly for wayward gear. Look at the spot where you got your water. You may find a spoon, cup, or even a cooking pot sitting there.

Of course, you want to leave a clean camp. Pick up wrappers or other scraps even if you were not the one who dropped them. There is no reason others who follow should not have the same enjoyment you did from your camp.

Chapter 9

GOOD MANNERS

On Display

When you are in a national park or forest you are on public display. It is public land. How you behave affects thousands of others who use or will use the same land.

For some reason, there are campers who are polite and well behaved in the privacy of their own homes, but when they are turned loose on public land they become crude, destructive, ill-mannered ruffians.

These are the types who paint messages on boulders, carve their initials in trees, line a trail with candy wrappers, and leave a garbage dump to mark their camp. Still worse are those who start rock slides deliberately, tear down or cut up trail signs, and pollute water supplies. Such behavior has no place in the outdoors. Such campers should be banned from the forest.

Perhaps it is pointless to devote a chapter to good camping manners. I am certain that the campers who rouse my ire either cannot or do not read. They never get the message. And, of course, most campers have enough sense to behave with dignity and respect for others. They do not have to be told how to behave in the outdoors.

There are, however, a few subtle points of good manners that novice campers sometimes neglect.

NOISE

Shouting, whistling, and loud conversation bothers neighboring campers and hikers on the trail. Save shouts and whistles as calls of distress, and keep your conversation down.

Singing and playing musical instruments around the fire at night is great fun, but it is not so much fun for nearby campers who are trying to sleep. If you plan an evening song-fest and you have close neighbors, at least invite the neighbors to join you. If they do not come to your fire, keep the volume down. Let them know you are aware of their presence.

Transistor radios are the bane of the outdoors, but some campers insist on bringing them and playing them. This can be hard on your fellow campers as well as your neighbors. If you must play a radio, keep the sound low. Better yet, use an earphone.

TRAIL ETIQUETTE

Do not crowd on a slower party of hikers and then rush through them without a word. The slower hikers will stop at a safe spot if you ask to pass.

Out of common courtesy, always speak to hikers you meet on the trail. For one thing, you might learn something about the country you are traveling into, and you will find that hikers are almost always in an open frame of mind, eager to swap stories and information.

Don't walk two abreast on a trail that was designed for one hiker at a time. This wears the trail wider than it need be, and on a hillside, you can accidentally start rocks rolling if you walk along the trail edge. Often you will see trails through a meadow that branch and weave with a confusion of sidetrails. The sidetrails mark unsuccessful ventures at shortcuts or places where several campers have walked side by side. Stick to the main trail and walk single file.

In rocky regions, particularly those once polished by glaciers, you may come to trails that are difficult to trace. Sometimes these are marked by cairns, two or three stacked rocks. If you find cairns that have fallen, rebuild them; and it is a good idea, after you have negotiated a faint trail with difficulty, to back-track for a few minutes and build fresh cairns. This will guide those who follow you.

Of course, you must never tamper with trail signs, and if you find signs that have been damaged, report them to a ranger when you leave the forest.

Certainly you will not discard food wrappers and other trash along the trail, but let's do something more than look at trail trash as we pass. Join the Bendover Club. This simply means stooping to pick up the offending piece of garbage. If the Bendover Club had a bigger membership, trail trash would be a rare sight.

I know, it is annoying to pick up someone else's garbage, but picking up a piece of scrap and stuffing it out of sight in your pocket will give you a smug feeling of righteousness that will help you forget your anger over seeing the scrap in the first place. Try it. You'll see that it works. And welcome to the club.

CAMP ETIQUETTE

You can be a member of the Bendover Club in good standing, or rather, bending, from work in camp as well as on the trail. You many have to do some picking up if you want a clean camp. Too many campers are thoughtless about camp litter.

There is another kind of litter which bothers me. These are the "improvements" that campers handy with a knife or hatchet like to leave behind. Poles wedged between trees as a table or bench are the most common works that these campers leave to posterity. I tear these things down and burn the poles in my fire. Who needs furniture on a camping trip?

You will undoubtedly come across the trail of the nail driver. This nut won't make camp until after he has driven at least one nail into every tree in sight. Some of the nails are used as clothes hangers and others for stringing lines, but this does not explain why so many nails have been used. Little can be done about the nail driver. Just be sure there is not one in your party. Incidentally, be cautious about putting these nails to your own use. They usually start pitch, which will make a mess on any clothes you hang on the nail.

FELLOW CAMPERS

If you go camping enough you will eventually have someone in your own party who annoys you, perhaps even spoils your trip. What do you do about it—or, rather, him or her, as the case may be?

First, remember that tempers do grow thin at the end of a long day. Perhaps what is annoying you is just a trifle which you can forget in the morning. Make sure, in other words, that the problem is not simply lack of patience on your part.

But things will happen that no amount of patience can tolerate.

The food thief will probably be the camper you want most to strangle. This person gets into the main food supply, usually when no one is looking, and nibbles away. When caught, the food thief will say he was just taking a little bit. Usually, it turns out that he has taken "a little bit" about twenty times, and you and your friends may spend the final day of your trip on short rations.

Another camper who will drive you slowly mad is the complainer. This person can find something wrong with anything and everything. He usually starts out complaining about the route that everyone has already agreed upon. Then he will complain about the food. Next, if he sees a cloud, he will start to work on the weather.

Sometimes, if the complainer has a sense of humor, you and your friends can break him of his habits with a little concentrated kidding, but watch out if he can't laugh at himself. He may next complain that everyone is picking on him.

The lazy camper who won't do anything until he's asked and then goes to work with slow reluctance can make your trip unpleasant. He is perfectly content to let others haul water, gather wood, cook, and rig tents. You can sometimes get action from this fellow by cutting him out of the benefits. If he misses a meal because he did nothing to help prepare it, chances are he will be a willing helper next time.

The late sleeper is closely related to the lazy camper, but he is easily cured. If a late sleeper has delayed the start of your hiking day just once, it is time to act. You and a friend simply hoist the foot of the late sleeper's bag and tumble him out. It is very effective, sometimes amusing, and can be repeated as many mornings as necessary.

The break-down camper is the one who is always having trouble with his pack, his boots, or some other vital piece of gear. You have to stop and wait while he makes repairs. Naturally, anyone can have trouble once in a while. But the break-down camper has things going wrong time after time. Either he has the wrong gear, hasn't checked it properly in advance, or does not know how to use or adjust it.

At the other extreme is the gear-bragger. Everything this fellow has is either the best or the most expensive, and he wants everyone to know about it. This fellow can be galling, particularly when you are still trying to save for a modestly priced packframe and bag and have to get by with an old rucksack. You can sometimes kid these fellows into more modest talk, but usually they have very little sense of humor.

The risk-taker is a danger to all in your party. He will try to do fool things such as climb over steep rocks or dance across a log bridging a stream. When these fellows get hurt, it changes your status from campers to rescuers. Sometimes the risk-taker can put you in danger as you try to rescue him.

Of course, all of the above will not be in your party at the same time. One is enough. Often there is little you can do about a troublemaker, except, when you organize that next trip, you can exclude him.

Chapter 10

PLANNING A TRIP

The Key Questions

In a way this whole book has dealt with planning a trip. We have talked at length about what you need to know and what you need to have, but as you might suspect, planning a specific trip brings us down to some specific details we have not yet said much about.

Before you can begin to plan a trip, you must have answers to some key questions. Who will go? How many will go? And where will you go?

Obviously, if your party includes hikers who have never carried a pack before, it is going to affect your planning. This is true if there is just one novice in the group. You have to figure on short daily marches, and in some cases, you or a camper with more experience should check over the beginner's gear before the trip to make sure it is complete and in good order.

You cannot begin to plan meals and start repacking food until you know how many are going to be in your group. And numbers are significant in other ways as well. We will talk about this in a moment.

Where you go, the type of terrain you will have, the altitude, the weather, the availability of water—all influence planning.

Let's talk about the key questions separately, but first I want to emphasize the importance of sticking with a decision. Suppose five of you agree on a trip. The food is bought and repackaged for individual meals—five servings in each package. Then, the day before you start, someone invites a sixth camper to come along. Do tempers rise? Are there some hard feelings? You can bet there will be.

Again, suppose your group has agreed on where you will go a good month before the trip is to begin. Someone, undoubtedly, has taken the trouble to write for maps and information. Certainly you have a daily schedule worked out, including the number of miles to be hiked each day, where your camps will be, and whether or not there will be day-long layovers for rest, fishing, or other nonhiking activities. The day before the trip is to begin, some in your group get the idea that they want to go someplace else. Again, you can be sure that there will be some heated arguments.

Last-minute changes should not be part of the planning process. It is true, you may have a member of your party drop out because of sickness or some unforeseen obligation, but a reduction in numbers is not as serious a problem as an increase, and besides, you can often find another camper to take the dropout's place.

WHO?

This may be your most difficult question to answer. This book cannot begin to tell you how to choose your friends. In fact, choosing friends is such a personal matter that any generalities would almost certainly be useless.

However, we can say this: Know your fellow hikers. Later

in your camping career you may sign up with a hiking group or club that organizes special trips. On these trips you will often find yourself with a party of total strangers. This can be an excellent way to meet new friends, but it is not a good experience for a beginner who is still learning the basic arts of backpacking.

With friends, you can help each other work out problems together and no one will be overly worried about showing his inexperience or lack of confidence. I should say with *most* friends. As you know, there are characters who like to pretend they know everything, and there are others who like to criticize and tease. But here we are, getting into that difficult problem of choosing friends. The point is, if your friends have some annoying traits, you should be well aware of these traits beforehand. Discovering them when you are trying to light your first campfire in the wilds or trying to rig a tarp shelter in a windstorm can be a very unpleasant surprise.

In selecting your fellow campers, it is a good rule to choose friends of nearly equal physical development and stamina. A hiker who cannot keep up with the others, who cannot carry his fair share of the gear and groceries, will slow everyone down, and you can be sure that the slower or weaker hiker will not enjoy the camping trip. He will not only tire quickly, trying to keep up, but he will also feel embarrassed and guilty about making others wait for him.

The above does not mean that you should avoid inclusion of an older or more experienced hiker in your group. If an old hand is willing to join your group, by all means, welcome him eagerly. There is no quicker way to improve your camping skills than having an experienced camper in your party. Incidentally, a good camper never stops learning.

If possible, the members of your party should have similar interests; at least, interests should not conflict. For example, if half the party wants to devote all spare time to fishing while the other half wants to explore or perhaps climb a peak, you may have serious problems. Often these various interests can be worked out in the planning stage, provided everyone makes their interest known well in advance. For instance, you can plan a free day when your peak climbers can do their thing, and usually you can arrange it so that the camp for that free day is next to a good stream that will satisfy the fishermen in the party. What you want to avoid are factions that arise after a trip begins, factions that argue over the schedule and try to change your carefully laid plans.

You will not ordinarily have much difficulty with conflicting interests if you keep your party small. This leads to the next key question in planning.

HOW MANY?

If it is not already obvious, let me state clearly that I recommend small groups for your first backpacking trips. The bigger the number, the greater the complications both in planning and in the trip itself. By small groups, I mean two or three.

Some of the experts say that the minimum number for safety is three. The idea is that if one hiker is injured so badly that he can no longer walk, a second hiker can stay with him while the third goes for help. This undoubtedly is sound for backpacking in remote regions where it may take two days to hike out for help. Your first trips, however, should not take you so far from civilization. Help should be well within a day's hike. Thus, you will not have to leave an injured hiker alone through the night. Certainly, accidents will happen, but I do not agree that a party of two should be avoided for short trips.

You and one trusted friend will have an easy time sharing camp chores, splitting loads, agreeing on plans, even changing plans, if necessary. In a party of three or more, such simple decisions can often lead to arguments. And there is often a tendency for factions to form with three or more campers. But, you say, we're all friends. We always get along fine. This may well be true in normal life, but stresses rise easily among a tired group of campers. I have seen campers argue at length over the selection of a campsite. I have even taken part in these arguments and realized too late that the whole debate was ridiculous. If there are factions in a group, you may find yourself arguing over many things of small importance. This is because the factions, once formed, tend to disagree about everything.

What about solo camping? Beginners should not attempt it. You can become sick. You can be immobilized by an injury, and no matter how careful you are there is still a risk of injury. Only after you have camped for several seasons should you consider solo camping, and even then, consider it very carefully and be sure to make that first solo trip a short one. I must warn you that the greatest danger of solo camping is loneliness. We are social animals. The isolation that descends upon a solo camper in the wilderness is complete, something very few can handle with comfort.

Veteran backpacker Colin Fletcher advocates solo camping. But he is unique in his self-sufficiency. The man revels in solitude and makes a good case for it in his excellent books. His point is that you can carry caution too far. You could even argue that one should never go any place alone. But Fletcher admits that solo camping is not for everyone. Also, he avoids unnecessary risks and makes sure that responsible friends know where he is going and when he is expected to return. Needless to say, he has years of camping experience behind him.

What about parties of three or more? Though I believe two is the ideal number for those first trips, you can have very successful trips with larger numbers. There is one difficulty that novice campers often want to ignore. You will have a greater chance for success with a leader. Sometimes, even if there are just three of you, you will be better off with a leader. Certainly when a party reaches five or six and more, a leader is vital.

One person has to see to the organization and execution of a trip. Certainly there are cases, particularly among experienced campers, where a leader is not necessary. Responsibility can be divided. One camper can see to the purchase and packaging of food. Another can collect the common gear, such as a camp stove, cooking pots, and shelter. Another can be responsible for transportation to the trailhead. Still another can collect maps and information about the camping area, and so on. But these would be campers who have been through it all before, who understand the importance of what they are doing and know how to get things done.

With beginners, you can hardly share responsibility and expect everyone to meet that responsibility without fail. Someone has to oversee both the preparation and planning, and handle decisions on the trip itself. This is important. How do you select a leader? This is difficult.

You want a camper who can use authority without abusing it. You must have someone whose judgment you respect. At the same time, you and your friends certainly do not want to be bossed needlessly. Finding someone who has the leadership ability and is willing to take on the responsibility is sometimes impossible. If you should be stumped in your search, I suggest that you reduce the size of your group, cutting it into two or perhaps three separate camping parties.

However, I do not suggest by this that you give up too quickly in your quest for a leader. And I do not believe in the old adage that leaders are born and not made. In fact, if leadership responsibility should fall on you, you will learn more about camping in that one trip, perhaps, than in all your previous trips. Remember, leadership and popularity do not necessarily go hand in hand. A camper who is popular because of his high spirits, his good singing voice, or his ability to tell funny stories can fail as a leader. Selection of a leader should not be a popularity contest.

One more word before we leave the leader problem. Give him or her your support. Once you have made your decision, either by formal vote by the group or by informal agreement, do not challenge each decision he or she makes. By cooperating fully, your group will make the job of leader an easy one, and if your leader lacks experience and has faults, chances are your trip will run smoothly just the same when all cooperate.

WHERE TO GO?

One common complaint among beginning backpackers is that there is no place to go. This is a fallacy. Even if you live in the heart of a densely populated area, a little research will show you that there are public lands and hiking trails no more than a day's drive or bus ride from your home. In fact, in the western region of the United States, you will have such a wide choice of camping areas that it will be difficult for you to make a decision. There are state and federal parks, National Forest Service lands, land under control of the Bureau of Land Management and National Monuments.

And do not overlook private farms or ranch land. Of course, you must always have permission from private-property owners to camp on their land. I prefer to have this permission in writing. There are some property owners who will refuse permission, but a surprising number are happy to grant it, particularly if they have a chance to meet you and see that you are a responsible person.

There are a few obvious rules. If you open a gate, close it behind you. Avoid livestock, and take pains to keep from startling sheep or cattle into minor stampedes. If there are dairy bulls in a pasture, stay out of that pasture. Owners almost always warn of such dangers when they grant permission. Of course, you must not mark your camp with garbage or chopped trees, and it is a good idea to bury your fire ashes. An owner who cannot find where you camped will be happy to let you use his property again.

Actually, few backpackers use private property because there is so much excellent public land. The U. S. Forest Service alone, with 154 National Forests encompassing a total of 182 million acres, maintains 165,000 miles of trail. Of the total acreage, 14.5 million has been placed in wilderness areas. These areas, with no man-made improvements other than the trails, are a backpacker's delight.

True, the wilderness areas are mostly west of the Mississippi, but even if you live in New York City, you can find good hiking and camping in the Catskill Mountains, just three hours away by car. In addition, there are the White Mountains north of Boston, and the Blue Ridge Mountains just a two-hour drive from Washington, D.C. The South Jersey pine barrens are practically on the doorstep of our biggest metropolitan area.

Vermont's 225-mile Long Trail, and the 1,995-mile Appalachian Trail, which connects with it, have kept thousands of Eastern hikers happy through many seasons. You can obtain information on the Long Trail by writing the Green Mountain Club, Inc., Box 94, Rutland, Vermont, 05701. For information on the Appalachian Trail write to the Appalachian Trail Conference, 1718 N Street, N.W., Washington, D.C. 20036.

In the West, the most famous trail stretches 2,156 miles along the Pacific Crest from Canada to Mexico. It is the main artery of a network of trails covering the Sierra Nevada. For information on the Pacific Crest Trail write to the Regional Forester, Region Six, either at 319 S.W. Pine Street, Portland, Oregon 97208, or at 630 Sansome Street, San Francisco, California 94111.

The Appalachian and Pacific Crest trails have been designated as national scenic trails. Fourteen others have been designated by Congress for possible inclusion in the scenic-trails system. They include the 3,100-mile Continental Divide Trail from Canada to within a few miles of the Mexican border, the Lewis and Clark Trail from Wood River, Illinois, to the Pacific shore in Oregon, and the Natchez Trace from Nashville, Tennessee to Natchez, Mississippi. Current information on these trails is available at the Bureau of Outdoor Recreation, Department of Interior, Washington, D.C. 20240.

Further information about camping areas can be obtained by writing regional offices of the national forests and parks listed in the appendix. In addition to the forest and park lands, there are 718,750 acres under the jurisdiction of the Bureau of Land Management. There are 135 separate regions in eleven western states under the bureau's management. Generally, these regions can be described as land that has not yet come under forest or park jurisdiction. Regional bureau offices are listed in the Appendix, but you can also obtain information by writing to the Division of Information, United States Bureau of Land Management, Washington, D.C. 20240.

Most of the information available through the various government offices, I should warn you, will be general information.

You need details, and you must have current information. Thus, it is a good policy when you reach a camping region to make a brief stop at the local ranger station or management office before you head into the hills. Tell a ranger your plans and ask if there are any specific problems.

Recently, when camping in the Mendocino Forest, which I know well, my friends and I saved a half day of fruitless driving and frustration by spending a few minutes with a ranger. The road we planned to take had been washed out several miles from the trailhead. It did not take long for us, helped by the ranger, to map out a trip from a different trailhead.

MAPS

In all your requests for information about a region, you should ask for maps. The national-park maps, given free to the public, are generally of too small a scale to be of much use to backpackers. Forest Service maps, also still given free, have much more detail than the park maps, and the scale is usually two miles to the inch. This means that one inch on the map represents an actual distance of two miles.

The Forest Service maps have one major fault. They do not show terrain. Sometimes they even omit elevations of major peaks and ridges. The best way to show terrain is with contour lines. If there is a difference of, say, forty feet in elevation between each line of contour, you can tell very quickly if a trail will be steep or level. If the trail crosses a section where the lines are crowded together, you know that the hike will be a steep one. By counting the lines and multiplying by forty, or whatever the contour interval happens to be on your particular map, you can even figure how many feet you must climb from the bottom to the top of a steep trail. If the trail crosses a region of few contour lines—it will appear almost blank on the map—you know that your walk will be practically level.

The best contour maps are made by the U. S. Geological Survey. They are available in several scales. The largest scale is two thousand feet per inch. It is referred to as a 7.5 minute map. This is because the maps are sectioned off by degrees, minutes, and seconds of longitude. Each 7.5 minute map thus covers 7.5 minutes of longitude on the earth's surface. Scales, actually, are given in the map key in terms of a fraction. The 7.5 minute map scale, for instance, is represented as 1/24,000. You must divide the bottom figure by twelve to convert this to an inch-per-foot ratio. The next smaller scale is 1/62,500 on what is called the 15 minute map. This translates to 5,208.33 feet, just 71.67 feet short of a mile, per inch. The survey's maps for Alaska, by the way, have a 1/63,360 scale, which comes out to exactly a mile per inch. The survey has three smaller-scale maps with scales of about two, four, and sixteen miles per inch, but most hikers prefer the 7.5 or the 15 minute maps because of their great detail.

For maps of regions east of the Mississippi you should write to the U. S. Geological Survey Service, Department of Interior, Washington, D.C. 20240. For maps west of the Mississippi, write to the Geological Survey, Federal Center, Denver, Colorado 80200. You will be sent a map catalog from which you can order the maps you wish. All but the two smallest-scale maps can be had for fifty cents each. The four-mile map costs seventy-five cents and the sixteen-mile maps costs a dollar.

For maps of camping areas in Mexico, write to Direction de Geograpiay Metrologia, Tecubaya, D.F., Mexico. Ask for maps of the Mexican national parks and forests, describing the region that interests you. For Canadian maps, write to the Canadian Government Travel Bureau, Ottawa, Ontario, Canada, or to the Map Distribution Office, Department of Mines and Technical Surveys, Ottawa, Ontario, Canada.

In all your requests for maps and information, allow plenty of time for correspondence. As noted, you have to be sent a catalog before you can send in your order for contour maps, and often, as is typical in government operations, your request for information will be referred to branch offices or other departments.

Many outdoor-supply stores carry topographical (contour line) maps as well as guide books for specific hiking regions. The maps are often offered at prices slightly higher than those charged by the government, but the convenience makes up for this. Guide books, when available for your area, are excellent buys. They are loaded with information, and in some cases a trail will be described in such detail that you can plan your hike almost to the minute.

ROUTE PLANNING

With the map before you, you and your camping friends can decide how far you will travel each day of your trip. If you want to stop over for a day, you can decide when and where this stop will be, and if you want to make side trips, you can decide when and where these will take place. All these are important decisions. Everyone in your party should take part in making them. This may avoid debate and disagreement during the trip; at least, it should reduce debate.

We have already warned against trying to cover a great block of miles on your first day. I would say that about ten miles would be the first-day maximum, less than this if you face steep trails or are hiking in altitudes over six thousand feet.

Backpackers in good condition can cover between two and three miles an hour on level ground. On a steep climb it may take an hour or more to cover a mile. This is why a contour map is so valuable in planning a trip.

You will read about experienced backpackers who log twenty miles a day. This is hard hiking. Do not include any twenty-mile days in the schedule for your first trips. Wait until you are confident that you and your friends have the stamina for this distance.

In mapping out your route, there are really three basic choices. Perhaps the most satisfactory is the loop, in which you return to the trailhead by a different trail than the one you used to leave it. On a loop, you are constantly seeing new country. Often, however, you may not be able to plan a loop. You must go out and come back on the same trail. This is sometimes called the yo-yo route. The third choice takes some help. This is the pickup route. You have a friend with a car drop you off at the start of a trail, and then pick you up an agreed number of days later at the other end. This is very satisfactory provided you can find a willing friend. Of course, it forces you to stay on schedule.

In most regions, your map will show you the availability of water. However, in the Southwestern United States many of those blue stream lines on the map indicate seasonal water courses. They may be dusty gullies during the dry season of the year. You should check with rangers before starting your hike if you have any doubts about water supply.

SHARING THE LOAD

Let's talk about money before talking about pack loads. The expenses for a trip should be shared equally among everyone in your party. Perhaps one person is in charge of buying the food. He or she must keep a careful account of all that is spent so that you and your friends can cover the costs. Do this before you start your trip.

Regarding pack loads, you cannot expect everyone's pack to weigh the same. There are personal items of gear that vary with individual campers, but the common gear should be divided and distributed as evenly as possible among everyone in your party. Common gear includes the camp grate, cooking pots, food, tarps or tents, a stove and fuel, and the first aid kit. Often it is difficult to make equal divisions of all common gear, and many campers do trade personal gear such as spare clothing or a ground cloth to even things up.

WHEN TO PLAN

Planning, as you can see, takes time. So why not use the winter months to send for catalogs, information, and maps? When snow blocks the mountain trails, you and your friends can spend many happy evenings in a warm house, planning trips for the coming season. Planning is really part of the fun.

Of course, after you have a few seasons of backpacking behind you, you will discover that recalling past trips is as much fun as planning new ones. Each new trip adds new memories. In fact, backpacking is really nothing more than that—a simple way to add happy memories to your life.

But this is jumping far into the future. Right now, you are eager to hit the trail. It is indeed time to get started. Good luck and happy hiking!

BIBLIOGRAPHY

American Red Cross. *First Aid Textbook*. Garden City, N.Y.: Doubleday & Co., 1970.

Angier, Bradford. *Home In Your Pack*. New York, N.Y.: Collier Books, 1972.

———. *How To Stay Alive In the Woods*. New York, N.Y.: Collier Books, 1972.

———. *Skills For Taming the Wilds*. Harrisburg, Pa.: Stackpole Books, 1967.

———. *Wilderness Cookery*. Harrisburg, Pa.: Stackpole Books, 1960.

Bates, Joseph D. *The Outdoor Cook's Bible*. Garden City, N.Y.: Doubleday & Co., 1964.

Cardwell, Paul, Jr. *America's Camping Book*. New York, N.Y.: Charles Scribner's Sons, 1969.

Fletcher, Colin. *The Thousand-Mile Summer*. Berkeley, Calif.: Howell-North Books, 1964.

———. *The Man Who Walked Through Time*. New York, N.Y.: Alfred A. Knopf, 1968.

———. *The Complete Walker.* New York, N.Y.: Alfred A. Knopf, 1971.

Jansen, Charles L. *Lightweight Backpacking.* New York, N.Y.: Bantam Books, 1974.

Johnson, James Ralph. *Anyone Can Backpack In Comfort.* New York, N.Y.: David McKay Co., 1965.

Kjellstrom, Bjorn. *Be Expert With Map and Compass.* Harrisburg, Pa.: Stackpole Books, 1968.

Manning, Harvey. *Backpacking, One Step At a Time.* Seattle, Wash.: The Rei Press, 1972.

Merrill, W. K. *All About Camping.* Harrisburg, Pa.: Stackpole Books, 1963.

Muir, John. *The Mountains of California.* Garden City, N.Y.: American Museum of Natural History, 1961.

Rathmel, R. C. *Backpacking.* Minneapolis, Minn.: Burgess Publishing Co., 1964.

Riviere, Bill. *The Camper's Bible* (revised edition). Garden City, N.Y.: Doubleday & Co., 1970.

———. *The Complete Guide to Family Camping.* Garden City, N.Y.: Doubleday & Co., 1966.

Rustrum, Calvin. *The New Way In the Wilderness.* New York, N.Y.: Collier Books, 1973.

Starr, Walter, Jr. *Guide to the John Muir Trail.* San Francisco, Ca.: Sierra Club Books, 1967.

Sutton, Ann and Myron. *The Appalachian Trail.* New York, N.Y.: J. B. Lippincott Co., 1967.

Wood, Robert S. *Pleasure Packing.* Berkeley, Ca.: Condor Books. 1972.

Appendix

THOSE WHO HELP

Suppliers

There are a great many outdoor-equipment suppliers and the number increases each year. To keep this list at a reasonable length, I am naming only those firms which answered my requests for catalogs promptly.

Alpine Design
3245 Prairie Ave.
P.O. Box 1091
Boulder, Colo. 80302

Packs, clothes, tents, and sleeping bags. No food.

Antelope Camping Equipment
10268 Imperial Ave.
Cupertino, Calif. 95014

Packframes and bags.

L. L. Bean
Freeport, Me. 04032

Complete line except for food

Bishop's Ultimate Outdoor   Tents.
   Equipment
6804 Willwood Rd.
Bethesda, Md. 20034

Thomas Black & Sons   Complete line except for
930 Ford St.   boots and food.
Ogdensburg, N.Y. 13669

Camp Trails   Packs and tents.
4111 W. Clarendon Ave.
Phoenix, Ariz. 85019

Eastern Mountain Sports   Complete line except
1041 Commonwealth Ave.   for boots.
Boston, Mass. 02215

Frostline Kits   Do-it-yourself kits for
P.O. Box 9100   sleeping bags, tents, and
Boulder, Colo. 80301   clothing.

Holubar   Complete line except
P.O. Box 7   for food.
Boulder, Colo. 80302

Kelty Pack, Inc.   Packs with some clothing
10909 Tuxford St.   and specialty gear.
Sun Valley, Calif. 91352

Moor and Mountain   Complete line.
14 Main St.
Concord, Mass. 01742

Sierra Design   Clothing, cooking gear,
Fourth and Addison Sts.   sleeping bags, packs, and
Berkeley, Calif. 94710   tents.

Ski Hut   Complete line except
1615 University Ave.   for food.
Berkeley, Calif. 94703

Stow-A-Way   Complete line except for
166 Cushing Highway   boots.
Cohasset, Mass. 02025

National Forest Regional Offices

Ask for the booklet on the recreational areas in your region of interest.

Eastern Region
6816 Market St.
Upper Darby, Pa. 19082

Southern Region
50 Seventh St. N.E.
Atlanta, Ga. 30323

North Central Region
710 N. Sixth St.
Milwaukee, Wis. 53203

Alaska Region
Fifth St. Office Bldg.
Juneau, Alaska 99801

Northern Region
Federal Bldg.
Missoula, Mont. 59801

Rocky Mountain Region
Denver Federal Center
Bldg. 85
Denver, Colo. 80225

Southwestern Region
Federal Bldg.
Albuquerque, N.M. 87101

Intermountain Region
Forest Service Bldg.
Ogden, Utah 84403

California Region
630 Sansome St.
San Francisco, Calif. 94111

Pacific Northwest Region
P.O. Box 3623
Portland, Ore. 97212

National Park Regional Offices

Ask for booklets on parks in the region that you wish to visit. The supply is sometimes limited.

National Capital Region
National Park Service
1100 Ohio Dr. S.W.
Washington, D.C. 20242

Northeast Region
National Park Service
143 South Third St.
Philadelphia, Pa. 19106

Midwest Region
National Park Service
1709 Jackson St.
Omaha, Neb. 68102

Northwest Region
National Park Service
1424 Fourth Ave.
Seattle, Wash. 98101

Southwest Region
National Park Service
Box 728
Santa Fe, N.M. 87501

Western Region
National Park Service
450 Golden Gate Ave.
San Francisco, Calif. 94105

Bureau of Land Management Offices

Offices listed below are grouped by states. Address your request for information to the bureau office closest to the region of your interest.

Alaska—
555 Cordova St.
Anchorage 99501

516 Second Ave.
Fairbanks 99701

Arizona—
Federal Bldg., Room 204
Phoenix 85025

California—
Federal Bldg., Room 4017
Sacramento 95814

1414 Eighth Ave.
Riverside 92502

Colorado—
14027 Federal Bldg.
Denver 80202

Idaho—
323 Federal Bldg.
Boise 83701

Montana, North and South
   Dakota—
Federal Bldg.
316 North 26th St.
Billings, Mont. 59101

Nevada—
Federal Bldg.
300 Booth St.
Reno 89505

New Mexico, Oklahoma—
Federal Bldg.
Santa Fe, N.M. 87501

Oregon, Washington—
729 Northeast Oregon St.
Portland 97232

Utah—
Federal Bldg., Eighth Floor
125 South State St.
Salt Lake City 84110

Wyoming, Nebraska, Kansas—
2120 Capitol Ave.
Cheyenne, Wyo. 82001

Other States—
Robin Bldg.
7981 Eastern Ave.
Silver Springs, Md. 20910

INDEX

Though born in Los Angeles, RICHARD B. LYTTLE is really a product of rural California. He graduated from high school in Ojai, served in the Navy in the 1940s, and attended the University of California at Berkeley, where he majored in English and professed boxing as his sport. He graduated with a B.A. degree and several bruises.

Mr. Lyttle has worked as a cowboy, farmer, newspaper reporter, editor, bartender, and school-bus driver. He began selling stories and articles for children in the 1950s. He sold more than 150 articles before turning to books. This is his sixth book.

The author has retained an interest in sports, particularly sailing, tennis, track and field, bicycling, and baseball. He is an enthusiastic camper, backpacker, and trout fisherman.

Mr. Lyttle, his wife Jean, and their children live in Inverness, a small town north of San Francisco and next door to the Point Reyes National Seashore.